DATE			

Geronimo

AND THE STRUGGLE FOR APACHE FREEDOM

Alvin Josephy's Biography Series of American Indians

Geronimo

AND THE STRUGGLE FOR APACHE FREEDOM

Written by Russell Shorto

INTRODUCTION BY ALVIN M. JOSEPHY, JR.
ILLUSTRATED BY L.L. CUNDIFF

Silver Burdett Press

10 9 8 7 6 5 4 3 2   (Lib. ed.)
10 9 8 7 6 5 4 3 2   (Pbk. ed.)
Library of Congress Cataloging-in-Publication Data

Shorto, Russell.
Geronimo and the struggle for Apache freedom / by Russell Shorto.
p.   cm.—(Alvin Josephy's biography series of American Indians)
Bibliography: p. 130
Summary: Recounts the life story of the Apache chief who led one of
the last great Indian uprisings.
1. Geronimo, Apache Chief, 1829–1909—Juvenile literature. 2. Apache Indians—
Biography—Juvenile literature. 3. Apache Indians—Wars—Juvenile literature. 4. Indians
of North America—Southwest, New—Wars—Juvenile literature. 5. Indians of North
America—Southwest, New—Biography—Juvenile literature.
[1. Geronomo, Apache Chief, 1829–1909. 2. Apache Indians—Biography. 3. Indians of
North America—Southwest, New—Biography.] I. Title. II. Series.
E99.A6G3274   1989
970.004'97—dc19   88-33687
[B]   CIP
[92]   AC
ISBN 0-382-09571-5 (lib. bdg.)
ISBN 0-382-09760-2 (pbk.)

Contents

Although this book is based on real events and real people, some dialogue, a few thoughts, and several local descriptions have been reconstructed to make the story more enjoyable. It does not, however, alter the basic truth of the story we are telling.

Unless indicated otherwise, the Indian designs used throughout this book are purely decorative, and do not signify a particular tribe or nation.

Author's note:
The Apache creation myth used in this book is adapted from *Geronimo's Story of His Life*, ed. S.M. Barrett, Garrett Press, New York, 1969. The author would also like to acknowledge his indebtedness to Angie Debo's *Geronimo: The Man, His Time, His Place*, University of Oklahoma Press, Norman, OK, 1976, and to Morris Opler's article, *"Chiricahua Apache,"* in *Handbook of North American Indians*, vol. 10, *Southwest*, Smithsonian Institute, Washington, D.C., 1983.

Introduction

For 500 years, Christopher Columbus has been hailed as the "discoverer" of America. But Columbus only discovered America for his fellow Europeans, who did not know of its existence. America was really discovered more than 10,000 years before the time of Columbus by people who came across the Bering Strait from Siberia into Alaska. From there they spread south to populate both North and South America. By the time of Columbus, in fact, there were millions of descendants of the true discoverers of America living in all parts of the Western Hemisphere. They inhabited the territory from the northern shores of Alaska and Canada to the southern tip of South America. In what is now the United States, hundreds of tribes, large and small, covered the land from Maine and

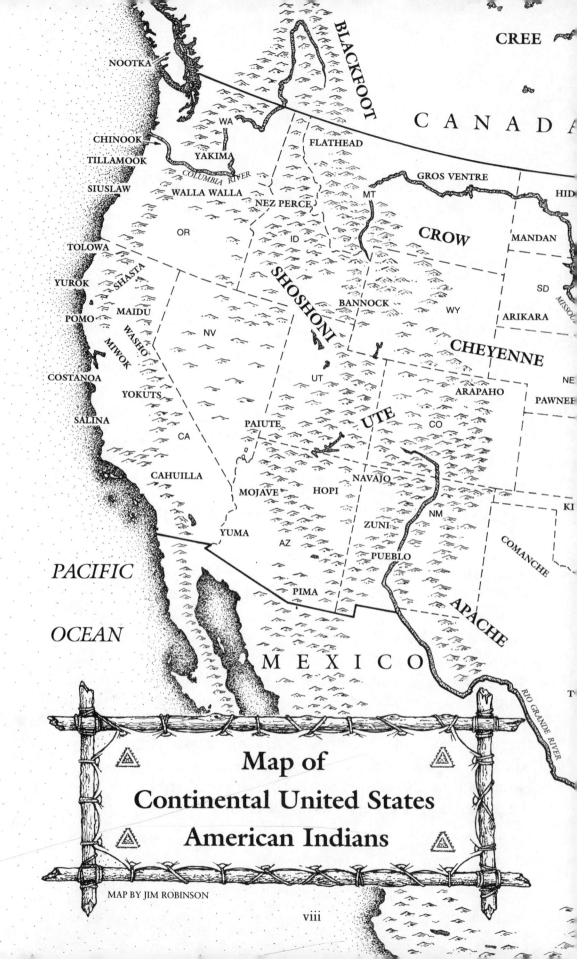

Map of
Continental United States
American Indians

Florida to Puget Sound and California. Each tribe had a long and proud history of its own. America was hardly an "unknown world," an "unexplored wilderness"—except to the Europeans who gazed for the first time upon its forests and rivers, its prairies and mountains.

From the very beginning, the newcomers from Europe had many mistaken notions about the people whose ancestors had been living in America for centuries. At first Columbus thought he had reached the East Indies of Asia, and he called the people Indians. The name took hold and remains to this day. But there were more serious misconceptions that had a tragic effect on relations between the Indians and the Europeans. These misconceptions led to one of the greatest holocausts in world history. Indians were robbed of their possessions, their lands, and the lives of countless numbers of their people.

Most Europeans never really understood the thinking, beliefs, values, or religions of the Indians. The Indian way of life was so different from that of the Europeans, who had inherited thousands of years of diverse backgrounds, religions, and ways of thinking and acting. The Europeans looked down on the Indians as strange and different, and therefore inferior. They were ignorant in the way they treated the Indians. To the white people, the Indians were "savages" and "barbarians," who either had to change their ways and become completely like the Europeans or be destroyed.

At the same time, many Europeans came as conquerors. They wanted the Indians' lands and the resources of those lands—resources such as gold, silver, and furs. Their greed, their superior weapons, and their contempt for the Indians' "inferior" ways led to many wars. Of course the Indians fought back to protect the lives of their people, their lands, their religions, their freedoms, their way of life. But the Europeans—

and then their American descendants—assumed that the Indians were all fierce warriors who fought simply because they loved to fight. Only in recent years have we come to see the Indians as they really are—people who would fight when their lives and freedom were at stake. People who were fun-loving children, young lovers, mothers who cried for the safety and health of their families, fathers who did their best to provide food, wise old people who gave advice, religious leaders, philosophers, statesmen, artists, musicians, storytellers, makers of crafts. Yes, and scientists, engineers, and builders of cities as well. The Indian civilizations in Mexico and Peru were among the most advanced the world has ever known.

This book gets beneath the surface of the old, worn-out fables to tell a real story of the Indians—to help us understand how the Indians looked at the world. When we understand this, we can see not only what they did, but *why* they did it. Everything here is accurate history, and it is an exciting story. And it is told in such a way that we, the readers, can imagine ourselves back among the Indians of the past, identifying ourselves with their ways of life, beliefs, and destinies. Perhaps in the end we will be able to ask: What choices would we have had? How would we ourselves have responded and behaved?

This is the story of Geronimo—one of the best-known Indians of the United States—and of his people, the Apaches of present-day Arizona and New Mexico. In some ways, Geronimo's story was a typical one. The whites who fought against him assumed that he was nothing more than a fierce and savage Indian. But Geronimo was a much greater man than this. With enormous courage, and against overwhelming odds, he struggled for as long as he could to save the lives and liberty of his people. When he surrendered and lost his freedom, white people began to understand Geronimo for who he really was, and opinions about him began to change. By the time of World War II, he had come to symbolize the struggle for freedom and the defence of one's nation. As American paratroopers leaped from planes into enemy-held territory, they shouted "Geronimo!" as a symbol of their courage and determination to carry out their mission.

—Alvin M. Josephy, Jr.

1
The Indian Exhibit

Visitors to the 1904 World's Fair in St. Louis, Missouri, had a lot to see and do. There were magicians, clowns, Ferris wheels, and wild animal shows. There were strangely dressed dancers from faraway places like Turkey and the Philippines.

But the biggest crowd of all was gathered around a small booth in a far corner of the fair ground. Compared to the other spectacular exhibits, this one didn't seem like much. It was simply a wrinkled old Indian. He looked rather dignified in his suit jacket and long pants. His hair was cut short and neatly combed and parted.

All day long this old fellow's booth was jammed with people eager to get a look at him and buy one of his photographs. He was, after all, the most

Geronimo

famous living Indian. Families would gather around excitedly. Fathers would point at him and tell their children how this wily old Indian, who now looked so calm and peaceful, had once terrorized the whole American Southwest, leading a band of vicious savages who slaughtered settlers just to see them die.

The children would shudder, and parents would calm them by assuring them that the Indian Wars were over now. All the Indians had been killed or locked on reservations, they would say, so America was safe now for civilized people.

Americans now believed that the Indians were a part of their country's past. The Indians' way of life seemed silly and primitive in the new age of telephones and electric lights. People at the World's Fair gathered around the old man and stared as if he were a crusted relic from a thousand years ago.

The old man would stare back and listen as people talked about him. He didn't understand their language, but he knew what they were saying. He knew that to them he was just a crazed old Indian who had killed their people for no reason. They didn't understand that his people, the Apaches, had lived free in the hot, windswept lands of the Southwest long before the American settlers came. It was the natural home of the Indians, not the Americans.

For centuries the Apaches had lived in small tribal villages on the dusty plains. They farmed in the lush valleys, and hunted among the high canyon walls. They had led a rambling life, moving often, like the animals they hunted. When invaders came, they held councils to discuss what was to be done. Before battle they often staged wondrous ceremonies to contact the spirits that they believed lived all around them. Then the warriors would smear on their warpaint and ride out to the attack.

And every evening, as the sun sank behind the desert cliffs and the plains turned from brown to black, the Apaches would raise their eyes to the crisp, starry skies and thank Usen, the maker of all things, for giving them a land that was perfect for them.

It was true that the old man, the last chief of his people, had been a fierce, proud warrior. He wasn't born a chief, but had earned the title through his bravery in battling American and Mexican soldiers. Because of his fierceness and love of freedom, the Apaches were one of the last Indian tribes to give in to the newcomers.

But in the end they did give in. All the members of his tribe who had not been killed in battle were rounded up and taken east to prisons. In time, as the fear of Indians faded, Americans became interested in them. The great leader was put on display for all to see. The warrior who had once led hundreds of war-frenzied braves into battle now sat in a booth as a curiosity. For twenty-five cents a customer could buy a photograph of him, and for fifteen cents more the old man would autograph the picture in large, wobbly capital letters: G E R O N I M O.

It was not the name he was born with. As an Apache child he was called Goyathlay. His childhood was spent roaming the pine-scented hillsides, playing with his friends while the hot sun beat down and summer thunderheads rumbled far off in the sky. Those days had been happy times for his tribe. Now, as he sat in his booth, the old man knew they were gone forever.

2
An Apache Child

The sun shone hot on the hard dusty ground, but the baby Goyathlay was safe in the shade. He was hanging from the branch of a shady tree in his *tsoch*, an Apache cradle. All day he watched the activity in the sunlight. There was a lot to see. Deerskin tipis sat like little pointed mountains on the dusty ground. Some boys led horses past Goyathlay in his tree. One of them had a stick and was tapping the first horse on the side. Two girls came up from the bank of the little stream that wound past the village. Water splashed out of their pitch-covered buckets and hit the ground, raising little clouds of dust. Behind the village, the canyon walls shot straight up into the sky. Up there an eagle soared on the wind.

The whole scene swayed in front of him as his cradle rocked from side to side in the wind. Just then a woman came from inside a tipi and walked toward him, smiling. She was a short, dark woman with bright eyes and teeth that flashed white when she smiled. She was his mother, Juana. As a little girl she had been captured by the Spanish—conquerors of Mexico and ancient enemies of the Apaches. She grew up among them and they gave her a Spanish name. When she talked to her infant son, it was sometimes in Apache and sometimes in Spanish.

The little boy in the cradle gave a small squeal of recognition and smiled at his mother. But the heat of midday and the rocking motion of the cradle were too much for him. As Juana knelt and took him from the cradle, he yawned and closed his eyes.

Apache cradle

Juana laughed and thought what a perfect name she had given her son. In Apache Goyathlay meant "Yawning One."

But Goyathlay was not destined to keep his name forever. As a baby it suited him, but as a man he would earn another name while fighting to avenge the horrible death of this woman who now held him close.

* * *

Goyathlay had three brothers and four sisters. Actually some of them were his cousins. Apache families were so close that any related children were often called brothers and sisters. To Goyathlay, the seven other children in the family that he grew up with were all his brothers and sisters.

The countryside was one big playground to these Apache children. One of their favorite games was hide-and-seek. Their parents encouraged them to play because the skills they learned in hiding from their playmates would become important to them as adult warriors. Goyathlay and the others would scatter across the rocky plains and choose hiding places behind yellow rocks and green pine trees. They would slither down along the banks of streams and rivers to conceal themselves. The seeker always moved in careful, silent, catlike strides.

The children also played at war. They would select a target to be the enemy. Sometimes they filled a sack with twigs and dead leaves. They would practice flying out from behind rocks and lunging at it. In this game, too, the adults encouraged them.

When they were tired of playing, they followed their parents into the green valley where the tribe's corn and melon crops were planted. There they would sit in the cool shade of the trees and watch their parents work in the gardens.

In the evening the families sat around their fires after dinner. Goyathlay's mother would tell him and his brothers and sisters stories of their religion. Apaches worshipped many spirits. They believed that everything in the world had a spirit, and that certain members of the tribe were blessed with the ability to contact the spirit world. Greatest of all was Usen, the unseen sky spirit, who looked over them. When he was an old man, Geronimo explained that he had been taught to pray to Usen "for strength, health, wisdom, and protection." But Apaches did not ask Usen's help to destroy their enemies. "We were taught that Usen does not care for the petty quarrels of men," Geronimo said.

Goyathlay's mother would often tell him the creation myth of the Apaches. It was a wild, enchanting story. Sitting around the leaping fire at night, warm and comfortable, their bellies full of food, the small Indian children would stare out into the inky blackness beyond the village and listen to the Apache story of the beginning of all things:

> *In the beginning the world was covered with darkness. There was no sun, no day. The perpetual night had no moon or stars.*
>
> *There were, however, all manner of beasts and birds. The human tribes could not grow in this dark world, for the beasts and serpents ate all the human children.*
>
> *There were two tribes of creatures who lived in the dark world: the birds or the feathered tribe, and the beasts. The birds were organized under their chief, the eagle. These tribes often held councils. The birds said they wanted light admitted into the world. This the beasts repeatedly refused to do. Finally, the birds made war against the beasts.*
>
> *The beasts were armed with clubs, but the eagle had taught his tribe to use bows and arrows. The battle raged for many days, but at last the birds won. After the war was over, the birds were able to control the councils, and light was admitted. Now humankind could live and even*

prosper. Since the eagle had led the fight to bring light into the world, people ever after wore his feathers as emblems of wisdom, justice, and power.

Among the few human beings alive at that time was a woman who had had many children, but these had always been destroyed by the beasts. Whenever she was able to escape the beasts, the dragon, who was very wise and very evil, would come and eat her babies.

After many years, a son of the rainstorm was born to her and she hid him away in a cave. The dragon had a suspicion that the woman had had another child, but he could never find him. In time, the child grew and was let out of the cave. One day, while he was hunting, the dragon discovered him. The dragon tried to kill the boy, but the boy shot the dragon through the heart with an arrow. With a great roar, the dragon rolled down the mountainside into a canyon far below.

This boy's name was Apache. As he grew, Usen taught him how to prepare herbs for medicine, how to hunt, and how to fight. He was the first chief of the Indians and wore the eagle's feathers as the sign of justice, wisdom, and power. To him, and to his people, Usen gave homes in the land of the west.

Goyathlay liked to imagine himself as the boy Apache, fighting the great battle with the dragon. One day, he told his family, he, too, would fight terrible opponents and win glorious victories.

Goyathlay's father smiled at this. He was Gray One, son of the great Maco, who had been an Apache chief. Gray One was very proud of his father, who had led the Apaches in wars against the Spanish. He told tales of Maco's bravery to his sons. Goyathlay, youngest of the boys, sat spellbound as his father talked. His mind filled with pictures of his grandfather charging on a great black horse, leading a band of war-painted

Apaches against Spanish troops. In the old days, Gray One said, there were many battles, and therefore much chance for bravery and honor.

When Goyathlay reached the age of eight his days of easy childhood were over. At this age boys and girls were separated and began learning their adult tasks. Girls gathered wood for fires, made clothes from animal skins, and learned how to cook and make medicines from wild plants.

Boys followed their fathers out across the dusty plains into the mountains. There they trained to become Apache warriors. Goyathlay's first day of training was something he had looked forward to for weeks. This training was very hard. But, remembering those times, the aged Geronimo said, "To me this was never work."

In his training a boy was told that his body must become like a weapon. He woke in the chilly, pre-dawn darkness and plunged into the river. Then he followed the warriors into the mountains. There he spent the long morning on his stomach, studying animal tracks. The boys were each given a mouthful of water and made to run up a mountain and back down without swallowing it. This, Goyathlay was told, was to teach them how to control their breathing while running in the hot southern mountains. To develop quick reactions, they dodged arrows that were shot at them. It was a harsh training, but it matched the harsh wilderness in which they lived.

The boys also learned how to survive alone in this wilderness and how to find their way. At the age of nine Goyathlay, now an intense boy with bright, fiery eyes, had reached an important stage in his training. As his father and mother watched, he was ridden out of the village behind a young warrior. They rode far into the mountains, along steep ridges and through wild,

desolate canyons, to a place Goyathlay had never been. There the young warrior set him on the ground and spun his horse around. With a cry he sped off, kicking up dust as he rode away.

Goyathlay was alone with no food, no horse, no water. He had been taught the ways of survival. If he had learned his lessons well, he would find his way back home. If he had not, he would die in the wilderness. Apache training was harsh.

The boy's trainers had not told Goyathlay's parents that they had taken him to an especially remote spot. They knew the boy loved a contest and had a bold, unstoppable spirit. These were qualities that might make a great warrior. They had to be put to the test.

Days later, at the hour when the sun was pulling long shadows from the trees, the boy walked quietly into the village. On his back was a bow he had made in the wilderness, and a quiver of arrows. Over his shoulder was the skin of a small antelope. He had killed it, eaten the meat, and used the skin for a blanket. In his eyes burned the fires of success, of victory over all the elements. Juana ran to him with a cry of joy. And Goyathlay, though he felt very grown-up, hugged his mother.

* * *

Maco, Goyathlay's grandfather, had been a chief, but this did not mean that Goyathlay would become one. The Apaches believed that the title of chief should not be passed automatically from father to son. Instead it should be earned through bravery and leadership. If Goyathlay were to become chief someday, he would have to earn the honor.

Maco had originally been chief of another band of Apaches, but he had married a woman of Geronimo's band and had come to live with them. The Apaches were divided into several tribes, and these were further divided into bands. Each band was a group of several families who lived and worked together. Goyathlay's band was called the Bedonkohe (pronounced bee-DON-ko-hay) Apaches. Maco's people were the Nednai Apaches, who lived in the high Sierra Madre Mountains of Mexico.

East of the Bedonkohe lands lived the Mimbreno Apaches. The chief of the Mimbrenos was the greatest of all living Apaches. His name was Mangas Coloradas. To Goyathlay and all the youths of the tribe it was like the name of a god. The Mimbreno Apaches lived about fifty miles from the Bedonkohes. It was fifty miles of rough, mountainous travel, so the tribes rarely visited. The boys of the Bedonkohe band had never seen Mangas Coloradas in person, though all their lives they had heard of his deeds.

There were two other Apache bands that were friendly with the Bedonkohes. The Warm Springs Apaches lived farthest east of all. They were named for their homeland, for the springs that were the lifeblood of the band. The other band, known as

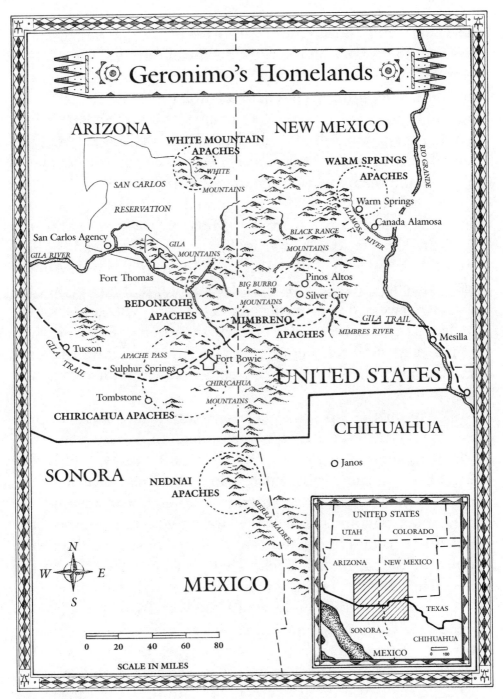

MAP BY JIM ROBINSON

the Chiricahua (pronounced chi-ri-KA-wa) Apaches, lived in harsh southern lands close to the Mexican border.

Actually, most of these bands considered themselves part of the Chiricahua group. They had a common heritage. All spoke the same language and held the same beliefs. All lived in tipis or in dome-shaped, brush-covered dwellings called *wickiups*. They hunted deer and antelope, and collected the same wild plants for food and medicine. They were good friends.

All of these Apaches also shared a history of warfare against the Spanish conquerors of Mexico, and later against the Mexicans. For hundreds of years Spanish and Mexican soldiers and raiders had ridden into Apache lands to find slaves. Almost every Apache had heard the thunderous sound of horses' hooves as raiders swept down on the tipi or wickiup villages. They all carried terrifying memories of their men being shot and their women and children being roped together to start the long march south. There these once-free people would live out their lives as slaves.

Early on the Apaches had learned to guard against these invasions. Whenever a village was raided, an Apache war party would assemble and fly south like a deadly wind, minds and hearts bent on causing as much pain as they had received. Living in the harsh deserts and among the cruel mountains—where bears, mountain lions, and snakes were frequent enemies—had made the Apaches fierce and clever. They could read the desert floor like the pages of a book. They could smell water on the wind. They could travel fifty miles in a day to destroy an enemy.

For centuries this warfare had gone on. By the time he was a teenager, Goyathlay had heard dozens of stories of Mexican horrors. He was told how the brave Apaches always struck back mercilessly. To the Apaches war was honorable, and a swift, brutal attack was a thing of great glory. To the Mexicans in the region the very word "Apache" struck terror.

As the centuries of fighting wore on, lawlessness grew among some of the Apaches. They took to raiding Mexican towns not just for revenge, but for supplies. They had discovered that the Mexicans made many useful things, and raiding was the simplest way to get them.

These periods of lawlessness were broken by cries for peace. Various Apache leaders would proclaim an end to the raiding and a return to their peaceful life. For a while things would be quiet. Then a stray Mexican or Apache party would go off on a raid, and the other side would strike back. A time of battle would begin again.

The Apaches were respected and feared by other Indian tribes in the area as well. Hopis, Navajos, Pueblos, and Zunis also lived amid the deserts, canyons, plains, and valleys of what is now the American Southwest. These were more settled tribes. The Hopis, Pueblos, and Zunis lived in permanent, apartmentlike structures made of adobe. The Navajos were farmers and weavers. To them the Apaches, terrifying warriors who moved across barren mountains with incredible swiftness, were a breed apart.

Goyathlay and the children he grew up among would have been surprised to learn how terrifying others thought their tribe. Of course, they were proud of their skills in battle, but to them war was only one part of life, and a distant one at that. Their childhood was a time of peace for the Apaches. They knew only of the battles of the past. As Goyathlay neared the age when he would be tested as a true warrior, he wondered whether the days of warfare were over for good. Perhaps, he thought, peace was here to stay.

It would be some years yet before he would see his first white man.

3

An Apache Warrior

O ne day in early autumn, Goyathlay stood amid a crowd of his Bedonkohe neighbors watching as a dust storm far out on the desert floor steadily approached them. As it neared Goyathlay saw that it was not a storm at all, but a large band of Indians. The Bedonkohe Apaches watched excitedly. Their friends, the Nednai Apaches, were coming to visit.

The Nednai had come far. From their mountains in the deep south they had walked and ridden more than 200 miles of harsh terrain, simply to visit their friends and relatives.

When the newcomers arrived, there was great excitement. Cooking fires were stoked and turkeys, deer, elk, and antelope roasted on spits. Pots of corn were boiled. Huge melons were stacked up, waiting to be cracked open. Goyathlay's mother and father greeted friends they hadn't seen in years. Women hugged each other. Men pointed to new scars and began telling the stories of how they got them.

The celebrations lasted for days. "By day we feasted," Geronimo remembered. "By night, under the direction of some chief, we danced." And after the dances it was time for games. Goyathlay was an intense competitor and loved all the games, even those he wasn't very good at. He often won by sheer determination. His favorites were wrestling and horse racing.

He was eager to show off his skills. He was the first Apache to challenge the Nednai boys to a horse racing contest. There were several very good racers among them, but Goyathlay won the race by yards. Everyone was impressed that one so young had such control over horses.

Alope

17

Goyathlay had a special reason for wanting to win so badly. There was a Nednai girl named Alope whom he had noticed at once. He couldn't keep his mind off her. He had smiled at her once or twice, but she just turned her head. He wanted to show her that Bedonkohe Apaches were the fastest and the strongest. Now he glanced again in her direction, but her soft eyes flashed quickly away.

Then one of the Nednais strode forward and challenged Goyathlay to wrestle. This boy was very strongly built, with a chest like a barrel and thick arms. His name was Juh (pronounced HOH). His father was one of the Nednai chiefs. He was a strong and good-looking boy, but he had a stutter. This, the Indians thought, was a sign of weakness.

Goyathlay and Juh fell immediately into a crouch and began circling like two cats. The crowd of adults and children backed away and began chanting. Goyathlay, smaller and thinner, kept his eyes fastened on his opponent. He watched and waited for an opening, for a chance to strike.

The next thing he knew, he was on his back, the hard earth beneath him, the wide sky above. Two eyes stared down into his. He felt the incredible strength of Juh's grip as he held him down. Goyathlay stared back, furious. He had a bad temper, and there was nothing that made him angrier than losing. Knowing that Alope had seen him be beaten nearly drove him crazy with fury. He clawed and tried to roll free, but the grip held him like a vice. The eyes smiled down on him maliciously.

There was nothing Goyathlay could do but admit defeat. The people cheered the victor, Juh. When the wrestlers stood up, Goyathlay nodded to show everyone that he had been beaten fairly. It was a rare thing for him, this sensation of defeat, and he did not like it.

Later Goyathlay got a chance for revenge. His sister Ishton had collected a basket of acorns from the forest and was

18

on her way back home with them. Juh and two of his Nednai friends saw her walking up the hillside and stole the basket from her. Goyathlay saw this happen. He ran after them and caught up with Juh at the riverside. There was another fight, and this time Goyathlay was the winner.

When Juh picked himself up his hair was dirty, and blood ran down his cheek. He stared hard into his opponent's eyes . . . and to Goyathlay's astonishment, he smiled! With that the two boys made peace. As solemnly as two old chiefs, they stood by the rushing river and swore by the mighty eagle that from this day forward Goyathlay of the Bedonkohe and Juh of the Nednai would be friends for life.

Then, looking up toward the village, they saw Ishton and Alope picking up the scattered acorns. As the two girls finished and headed for the village, Alope turned once toward Goyathlay and smiled.

Soon the Nednais returned home. Later that same year Goyathlay's ailing father died. Although he had been sick for some time, his wife, Juana, took it very hard. She wept as the watchers closed his eyes, painted his face, and wrapped him in a fine blanket. Gray One was laid in a cave high in the mountains, with his bows, arrows, and spears at his side. Goyathlay himself helped to block the entrance to the cave with stones.

"Wrapped in splendor he lies in seclusion," Geronimo said much later, "and the winds in the pines sing a low requiem over the dead warrior."

The death of Gray One meant that Goyathlay would take over the care of his mother. Although he was not yet a true warrior, he was now the man of the family.

His trial of manhood, which would make him a warrior, came soon after this. Juana, still feeling tremendous sadness at the loss of her husband, wanted to visit her friends among the Nednais. Goyathlay, Ishton, and several other children, as well

as some of the warriors and their wives, made the long journey
to the mighty Sierra Madres. Goyathlay rode fast. The picture
in his mind of Alope's face drove him on, making him both
eager and nervous.

Among the Nednais Goyathlay began serious training to
become a warrior. The Nednais, unlike the Bedonkohes, regu-
larly warred with the Mexicans. Other Apache groups often
joined them. Now, besides the Bedonkohes, several Mimbreno
warriors had come to join in the battles. Goyathlay was to be
taken with them on his first raid. His friend Juh, who was already a warrior, would be his guide.

Before leaving the village the young warriors stripped down
to their breechcloths and painted their faces for battle. As they
sat preparing themselves, an older man strode into the circle.
He was the tallest and noblest-looking man Goyathlay had ever
seen. As he came forward the warriors hushed. It was Mangas
Coloradas of the Mimbrenos, the greatest Apache chief. He
would lead them into battle personally.

He was even bigger than Goyathlay had pictured him. He
stood six-and-a-half feet tall, with gray hair flowing down onto
massive shoulders. His face was hard as steel, creased with age
and desert hardship.

Mangas Coloradas did not acknowledge Goyathlay, who
was only an apprentice. The boy would not be recognized until
he had proven himself as a warrior. As the apprentice it was
Goyathlay's job to take care of the horses and do the men's bid-
ding. He could not speak unless he was asked to. He had to
show that he was dependable and unmoved by the sight of human slaughter.

The warriors traveled for two days, sleeping in the heat of
the day and riding at night. At length they reached their desti-
nation, a large Mexican ranch. As they stripped for battle and

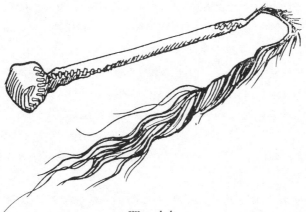

War club

smeared the red streak of warpaint across their cheeks, young Goyathlay's heart pounded like a drum. He knew that Mexicans were always eager to kill an Apache. The Mexican government offered one hundred dollars for an Apache scalp. But it wasn't fear that pumped the blood through his heart with such force. It was excitement.

Finally, they assembled. Mangas Coloradas's arm shot into the air, the signal to attack. Like arrows the Indians' horses swept across the plain toward the ranch house. Their throats strained with the fearsome Apache war cry. The Mexicans dashed outside, their rifles blazing.

It was a bloody encounter, as raids nearly always were. Several braves were killed. But many more Mexicans lay dead at the end of the fighting, and the Apaches dashed into the safety of the hills with the ranch's herd of horses in tow. The raid was a success.

It was Goyathlay's first battle. Although he had not been allowed to fight, he had proven himself able and dependable in assisting the warriors. Mangas Coloradas was well pleased.

After Goyathlay's fourth outing a ceremony was held in his honor. The number four had great importance in the Apache religion, so an apprentice warrior had to prove himself in four raids. Mangas Coloradas himself welcomed the young man into the brotherhood of Apache warriors. He sat before the dancing flames of the ceremonial fire with the great eagle-feather head-dress of the chief on his head. His broad shoulders gleamed with sweat. With his eyes closed, remembering the old words, the aging chief recited what would be expected of a new warrior. He must obey all senior warriors. He must fight with the brav-ery of an Apache.

Then, suddenly, the chief opened his eyes and looked at the youth for the first time. His hard mouth softened at the edges, and he nodded. With his mother watching, her eyes glistening in the firelight, Goyathlay thus entered manhood. It was the proudest day of his life.

Goyathlay was thrilled, but not just because he would now be able to join raiding parties. A man also had to be accepted as a warrior before he had the right to marry. The moment the ceremony was over he asked Alope to be his wife. Alope, her bright eyes dancing in the firelight, smiled nervously. She had been expecting this, but not quite so soon. Nevertheless, she accepted.

But her father still had to consent to the marriage. He agreed to give up his daughter in exchange for a herd of ponies. It was customary among the Apaches for a father to ask for something for his daughter's marriage. This, however, was a great deal to demand. "Perhaps he wanted to keep Alope with him," Geronimo guessed, thinking back, "for she was a dutiful daughter."

Goyathlay coralled the ponies himself in the next raid and succeeded in bringing them home. He formally presented them to the old warrior, who then gave up his daughter. This was all there was to the marriage ceremony among the Apaches.

When Goyathlay took Alope from her father's home, she became his wife.

At around this same time another couple got married, Juh and Goyathlay's sister Ishton. So now Goyathlay and Juh were bound even more closely together. They were truly brothers now. The two young warriors looked forward to fighting many battles together. Little did they know how powerful their enemy would be.

4

Goyathlay's Great Sadness

Goyathlay and his friend Juh had little knowledge of the wide world around them. To them the world was an endless expanse of dusty plains, shrub-covered hills, steep canyons, and high, green mountaintops. The people they knew about were the various Apache groups, the Mexicans, and a few other Indian tribes that occasionally passed through their lands.

They knew little about the vast "tribe" that was soon to change their lives. Two thousand miles east of the Bedonkohe homeland were places the Apaches could never have imagined. In cities like New York, Boston, and Philadelphia, thousands and thousands of people lived in buildings jammed side by side. They worked in factories and offices. They read newspapers, bought ready-made clothes, wrote letters, ate in restaurants, and did a hundred other things the Apaches would have been amazed by. Housewives were excited about an amazing new invention called the sewing machine. And some families were busy installing in their homes newfangled things called toilets.

But what was most impressive of all about these people was how many of them there were. At this time, in the 1840s, there were twenty million white Americans spread across twenty-eight states (compared to only about 6,000 Apaches in the Chiricahua groups) and more immigrants kept coming all the time. They came from Europe and Asia, from places where old customs and little land made it impossible for them to live decently. They poured into the cities of the American East.

Over the decade the East became more and more crowded. Fur trappers and adventurers spread the word about the rich, open lands of the West. Steadily, the new Americans started heading that way. They fanned out over the humid South, the icy Great Lakes region, and the endless Great Plains.

They wanted to go even farther westward, to conquer the whole continent from sea to sea, but there was a problem. The Mexicans were already there. Spain had colonized Mexico and much of the land from Texas to California. Now Mexico had won its freedom from Spain, and these northern lands belonged to it.

But in Washington, D.C., President James Polk was eager to stretch the boundaries of his country. He sent General Zachary Taylor and a detachment of soldiers to Mexico. Their job was to provoke the Mexicans into attacking them, so that the United States would have an excuse to declare war. The real reason for wanting war was so that America could capture those western lands. But the Mexicans refused to be led into this trap. So in 1846, President Polk declared war anyway.

By the time the war came, Goyathlay and the rest of the Apaches knew all about it. They knew that the Mexicans claimed the Apache homeland. They also knew that the Americans wanted ownership of it for themselves. To the Apaches this was amusing. The idea of owning land was as strange to them as the idea of owning air.

But that didn't mean they were unconcerned about who won the war. They were cheering for the United States, since every Apache was the sworn enemy of Mexico. To them, the United States was something vague and far off. If the Americans won, surely they would never be interested in coming thousands of miles to settle on a dusty patch of land. They would leave it to the Apaches, and all would be well. The Apaches felt sure of this.

In 1848, when Goyathlay was about twenty years old (he was never sure of his exact birthdate), the war ended. America had won and would now control 1,000 miles of land stretching from western Texas to California. This included all of the Apache homelands except for that of the Nednais. The Apaches in their tipis cheered the victory. They were very happy that the accursed Mexicans had been beaten. These Americans must be good people, they decided.

But soon they learned that the Americans had made a deal with their defeated enemies. The lands of Arizona and New Mexico were now in the hands of the Americans, who decided that the Indians who lived in those lands were their problem. The United States promised Mexico that they would keep the Indians from raiding Mexican towns. If any were caught doing so, the American soldiers would punish them. The Apaches didn't like this idea one bit. If they had quarrels with the Mexicans, what business was it of the Americans? They also weren't pleased to hear that the United States was sending an "Indian Agent" to keep the tribes in order. What was that all about?

* * *

For the time being, these happenings in the outside world didn't affect Goyathlay. He was busy with his new life. He returned to the Bedonkohe homeland with his mother and his new wife, and there he and Alope set up house. He was very proud of his first adult home. This is what he said about it:

"Not far from my mother's tipi I had made for us a new home. The tipi was made of buffalo hides and in it were many bear robes, cougar hides, and other trophies of the chase, as well as my spears, bows, and arrows. Alope had made many little decorations of beads and drawn work on buckskin, which she placed in our tipi. She also drew many pictures on the walls of our home."

Goyathlay and Alope were a well-matched couple. They each followed their responsibilities contentedly, and they lived as the Apaches had always lived. "We followed the traditions of our fathers and were happy," said Goyathlay. In time they had three children, "children that played, loitered, and worked as I had done," he said. Everything seemed perfect, and Goyathlay and Alope could have wished for it to last forever. But, as Apaches, they knew that nothing is forever.

It so happened that this was a time of peace between Apaches and Mexicans, and the Mexican state of Chihuahua (pronounced chi-WA-wa) was eager to keep up good relations with the Indians. The governor therefore invited the Apaches to come into the towns of the state and trade peacefully with the townspeople. Chihuahua is just south of New Mexico. Its neighboring state, Sonora, which is just below Arizona, still bore a smoldering hatred for the Apaches, and they were unwelcome there. As long as the Apaches stayed in Chihuahua, though, and didn't stray into Sonora, they would be welcome to do business.

This was good news to Goyathlay and all Apaches. The Bedonkohes excitedly prepared for the journey. This was to be a peaceful mission, a trip to the colorful markets of Mexican towns, so the men had decided that the whole band would make the journey. Goyathlay's wife, his mother, and his three small children accompanied him. The people loaded their ponies with hides of antelope, deer, cougar, and bear. These they would exchange with the townsfolk for colorful clothing, glass beads, knives, and other things they liked but could not make themselves.

Mangas Coloradas himself led them southward into Old Mexico. They traveled quickly, spurred on by their eagerness. Their first stop was a small town called Janos, where they planned to rest for a few days. Only the men went into the town itself. Just outside, they formed a large wickiup camp. They left some men behind to guard the camp, for the Apaches were always careful. But the guard only consisted of a few warriors, since they expected no trouble. Inside the camp the women and children waited eagerly for the men to return with the new supplies.

* * *

General Juan Carrasco, commander of troops in the Mexican state of Sonora, was a tough, wily veteran of many battles against the Apache people. To him Apaches were the enemy, pure and simple. When politicians talked of making peace with them, he just shook his head. He had seen them in battle. He saw them as vicious, wild, and uncivilized. As far as he was concerned, you couldn't make peace with them any more than you could with the mountain lions that occasionally attacked his men when they were trailing Indians in the mountains.

General Carrasco was authorized to hunt Apaches within the state of Sonora. But he and his men had become restless lately because the Apaches seemed to have abandoned the state. He decided to ignore the boundary and cross over into Chihuahua, just to check things out.

No sooner had he and his men done so than they came upon a whole Apache camp set up just outside the little town of

Wickiup

29

Janos. General Carrasco knew about Chihuahua's new policy of inviting Apaches to trade. He thought it was nothing more than an invitation to the Indians to come in and rob, raid, and kill. Sitting up on his horse, the general gazed out over the camp and smiled. He would take care of these savages. This would be child's play.

He glanced back at his lines of burly soldiers, their rifles ready. Unsheathing his sword, he pointed it at the sky, stood up in his stirrups, and sounded the charge.

* * *

Goyathlay and several friends were leaving the town when they were surprised to see two of their women running toward them. Their clothes were torn, and their faces were filled with horror.

"Soldiers . . . from another town," one of the women panted. "They attacked the camp, killed many of us, captured all our ponies, all the weapons and supplies. Many are dead. Many are dead." She fell into Goyathlay's arms, wailing.

Immediately the warriors, wary of a trap, separated and melted into the landscape on the outskirts of the town. They crept to the camp one by one, and found a sight that pierced their hearts. Their whole world was destroyed. The women they loved lay in pools of blood. Their small, innocent children were slaughtered, their arms and legs hacked off. Scattered fires were burning the last of their supplies. Moans drifted over the desolate site. What had been their happy camp was now a charred battlefield. General Carrasco had swept down on a village of women and children and slaughtered them like animals.

Goyathlay came upon a sight that would be burned into his mind forever. The bodies of his wife, his mother, and his children lay together in the dirt, horribly mutilated.

All the warriors felt the same agony. In one swift blow their families had been wiped out. No one shouted for revenge, though, and no one suggested taking off after the Mexican troops. They were all in shock, unable to believe what had happened.

Finally, Mangas Coloradas spoke. "There are only eighty of us here," he said, summoning the others. "We have no arms and we are deep inside Mexico, with Mexican troops all around us. We have no choice but to return home at once. We will think there."

With that the Indians turned and headed for home. But Goyathlay was unable to move. "I stood until all had passed, hardly knowing what to do," he said later, thinking back on that time of agony. "I did not pray, nor did I resolve to do anything in particular, for I had no purpose left. I finally followed the tribe silently, keeping just within hearing distance of the soft noise of the feet of the retreating Apaches."

A few days later the weary men, together with the few women and children who had escaped, reached their home. Goyathlay trudged to his tipi. When he saw it, tears ran down his cheeks. "There were the decorations that Alope had made," he said. "And there were the playthings of our little ones. I burned them all, even our tipi. I also burned my mother's tipi and destroyed all her property."

This moment of rage made him feel better, but only for a short while. For days he did not eat, sleep, or speak. The women tried to make him eat but he would not. He sat solid and immobile as stone.

Then one morning he rose and began walking. He did not know where he was going. He crossed the plain and headed into the mountains. Crawling on hands and knees, he scaled a treacherous peak. Climbing over the top he saw that he had come a different way to the cave where his father lay buried. Just outside the cave was a spring. Goyathlay knelt beside this stream, put his head in his hands, and cried. After a time he lay down beside the stream and looked up into the sky, thinking. He closed his eyes.

Suddenly, he thought he heard his name called: "Goyathlay . . ." He caught his breath and sat up. There was no one around.

"Goyathlay . . ."

There it was again. Was it real, or was he dreaming? It was a strange voice, airy and high-pitched, unlike any he had ever heard. It didn't sound human.

"Goyathlay . . ."

His eyes narrowed. That was the third call. Would there be another?

"Goyathlay . . ."

Yes, that was it! His name was called four times. Four, the Apache sacred number, was the symbol of the mystical Power, the force that came to certain Apache warriors at times of crisis.

"You will be strong," the voice told him. "You will avenge yourself, and all Apaches. No guns can ever kill you. I will take the bullets from the guns of the Mexicans. And I will guide your arrows. This you may believe."

Goyathlay shook all over. "I . . . I believe," he said. "I believe!" For the rest of his life Goyathlay would believe in the mysterious Power, the force that protected the Apaches. He would also believe that he could not be harmed by bullets. And, amazingly, through countless battles, raids, and skirmishes, he never was.

He ran down the mountain and into the village, shouting about what had happened. People nodded. They recognized the signs of the Power. This was clear confirmation that they were justified in what they were planning: revenge!

5

Becoming Geronimo

Goyathlay's news about the voice hastened the warriors to action. Mangas Coloradas planned a merciless attack on the troops of General Carrasco. He sent Goyathlay south to the Chiricahuas to ask for their aid.

Goyathlay met with Cochise, their great chief and second only to Mangas Coloradas in rank among the Apache chiefs. Cochise was a much younger man than Mangas Coloradas. At this time he was in his thirties, and in the prime of his strength. Like Mangas Coloradas, he was unusually tall for an Apache. He had large, round eyes that stared deeply into the eyes of others. He was known far and wide for his keen intelligence and his gentle ways.

Goyathlay sat across from him in his tipi, while Dostehseh, who was one of Cochise's wives and also the daughter of Mangas Coloradas, laid mescal cakes in front of them. A great warrior was entitled to have two or even three wives. By marrying his daughter to Cochise, Mangas Coloradas had strengthened the bonds between the two Apache bands.

Cochise was a leader of wisdom and feeling. As Goyathlay recounted the horrible slaughter of the innocent women and children, he saw the chief's stern face soften. Cochise felt the pain of his fellow tribesmen. He did not like the constant attacking that had gone on for so long between the Apaches and the Mexicans. But this horrifying deed, this senseless killing of almost an entire village, could not go unpunished. The Chiricahuas would join the war party led by Mangas Coloradas, Cochise told Goyathlay.

Goyathlay rode hurriedly back to give this news to Mangas Coloradas, then turned south again and headed toward Old Mexico and the lands of the Nednai Apaches. Juh had become the Nednai chief. He called a council of warriors at dawn. There, Goyathlay told all of the terrible fate of the Bedonkohes. The Nednais listened, awestruck, then gave their word that they would help to avenge the wickedness.

On a blustery autumn day of that year, 1850, the united Apache warriors stood outside the Mexican town of Arispe, prepared for war. They had marched into Mexico, traveling fourteen hours a day on foot and covering forty miles per day. They had traced General Carrasco's troops to this town.

The warriors were stripped to their breechcloths, cloths that could be worn like a skirt and then unwrapped and used as a blanket at night. In war the Apaches didn't like clothes choking their bodies, but preferred to feel the wind rushing against their bare skin. They wore mocassins on their feet and buckskin warbands around their foreheads. Across their cheeks and noses was streaked the red line of warpaint. All their hearts beat with

excitement as they stood on the windswept plain gazing at the town. They made no attempt to hide themselves.

They camped on the plain that night. They knew the Mexicans had seen them and would send their best soldiers out after them in the morning. Dressed for battle, the warriors held their war dance by the light of the fire. They chanted to the beat of an *esadadedne*, a sort of deerskin tamborine, preparing their minds for the coming battle. In the cold light of early morning they prayed to the mountain spirits to give them strong arms and keen eyes so that they would not fall into enemy traps.

Goyathlay was the most excited of all. Since he had lost more family than anyone else in the Mexican raid, the chiefs had decided to let him lead the attack. He was nervous but ready. As he later said, "I was no chief and never had been, but because I had been more deeply wronged than the others, this honor was conferred upon me, and I resolved to prove worthy of the trust."

The usual Apache method was to swoop down on the enemy then retreat, sending arrows from hidden perches. The warriors would change positions often so that the enemy could never count their numbers. But Goyathlay decided to meet the Mexicans head-on. He arranged his men into a semi-circle among the trees that lined the river. Here they waited, with their bows and the few stolen rifles they had ready.

Suddenly, a cry was heard from within the town, and a horn sounded. Two companies of infantrymen came charging across the plain toward them, followed by two companies of mounted cavalrymen. The infantry halted and fired into the main body of Indians. The Apaches began their deafening war whoop. The piercing cry met the rifle cracks, but the Indians held their fire.

Then Goyathlay gave the signal and the Apaches attacked. This was something the Mexicans hadn't expected. They held their places, though, and continued firing. Meanwhile, the arc of warriors descended on the rear of the Mexican forces. Goyathlay led the main charge, screaming like a demon as he ran, with tears streaming down his cheeks. Arrows flew from his bow and sunk with a thud into the chests of his enemies. All around him Apache warriors fell as bullets caught them, but he ran on. "In all the battle," he said, "I thought of my murdered mother, wife, and babies, of my father's grave and my vow of vengeance, and I fought with fury."

Suddenly, he realized that he was one of only four warriors left. The rest were either dead or had fallen to safety back among the trees. He had no arrows left, only his knife. Two soldiers appeared and shot two of the warriors. Goyathlay and his remaining companion made a dash for the trees, and the soldiers ran after them. Suddenly, Goyathlay's fury at the murder of his family came upon him once again. He fell to the earth and picked up the spear of a dead warrior. Spinning around, he lunged at his pursuer. Before the man could stop he was dead, the spear's shaft clean through his chest.

Now Goyathlay's eyes burned brighter. Alone on the field he lunged at the other soldier with his knife and tore into his heart. Bullets from the far line of soldiers sputtered in the dust all around him, but he had no fear of them, for he believed the Power had made him safe. He could hear the whoops and cries from his own warriors in the trees as they watched him with amazement. Goyathlay picked up the sword of the man he had just killed and waved it in the air madly. The Indians howled and cheered, drunk with the frenzy of battle.

The few Mexican soldiers left had retreated, so that this mad Indian was out of their rifle range. One stood up to charge closer for a shot. Goyathlay saw. He spun the sword over his head in a circle and charged too. The man saw the wildness and the hatred in his eyes. He crouched back down.

Now the Indians could hear the Mexicans talking. "San Jerome!" they cried, praying to St. Jerome to save them from this devil-Apache. The Indians didn't know the meaning of the cry, but they picked it up and began chanting to Goyathlay what they thought was the same call: "Geronimo! Geronimo!"

Goyathlay seemed to come to his senses now. Returning to his companions, he noticed that he was covered with the blood of those he had killed. His sticky fingers still held the sword tightly in his fist.

"Geronimo! Geronimo!" cried the warriors. The battle had been won. It would go down in history as the Apaches' greatest victory against the Mexicans. They had avenged themselves. They had a new war hero, and he, Goyathlay, had a new name. From this day on he would be known as Geronimo.

6

The Americans Arrive

The Apaches hoped their victory at Arispe would keep the Mexicans from bothering them for a long while. They wanted to be able to live in peace now. True, there were some newcomers on their lands. Settlers on their way to and from California had decided to stay in the new territory of New Mexico, which included Arizona and New Mexico. But the Indians were fairly certain that these scattered miners and farmers would not cause problems.

Geronimo saw his first Americans at this time. They were not settlers, but engineers and government officers who were drawing the new boundary between Mexico and the United States. Geronimo was a respected warrior now, whom many young warriors looked up to. He had heard that there were

Americans to the south, and he and several of these young men rode down to see what they looked like.

The boundary officials were uneasy when they saw a line of Apaches approaching them on horseback. But as they drew near, Geronimo held up his hand in a gesture of peace. He approached and spoke, but none of the men could speak Apache. Nevertheless, he later said, "We made a treaty with them by shaking hands and promising to be brothers."

The Indians camped near the officials, and the two parties had a friendly trading session. "We gave them buckskin blankets and ponies in exchange for shirts and provisions," said Geronimo. He and the other Indians liked these men and stayed with them for many days. "They were good men, and we were sorry when they had gone on into the west," he said. "These were the first white men I ever saw."

Over the next few years, though, American settlers continued to pour into the Apache lands, and problems arose. The Americans did not ask the Apaches' permission to settle on their lands. In fact, they treated the Apaches as if *they* were the invaders. Then there was a rash of horse stealing by Apaches and by Navajos who were passing through. This angered the settlers. Also the old hostilities with Mexico began to surface again.

One man did try to solve the problems. His name was John Greiner. He was the Indian superintendent whom the Americans had said they would send after the Mexican War had ended. At his request Mangas Coloradas went to Santa Fe to discuss the problems between the Apaches and the Mexicans. Mangas Coloradas told of the killing at Janos. He also described another time when Apaches were trading peacefully in Chihuahua. Mexican men pretending to be traders came with a supply wagon that had a cannon concealed in it. When the

Apache families gathered round to look at the goods, the cannon fired on them, killing many. "How can we make peace with such people?" he asked.

Superintendent Greiner saw the Apaches' point. A treaty, he said, was the only way to solve the problems peacefully. He drew up a treaty that would guarantee tribal boundaries. It promised the United States would punish those who harmed the Indians, and it forbade the Apaches from raiding in Mexico. Mangas Coloradas signed the treaty. This paper, Greiner told him, would settle the problems with the Mexicans, and would guarantee peace between the Apaches and the United States forever. Mangas Coloradas left the meeting feeling very good. He believed this man, for he had no reason not to. This was his first encounter with an American official.

* * *

Geronimo, meanwhile, had slowly adjusted to the loss of his family. He had married again, twice. His two wives were a symbol of his high standing in the tribe, and he was proud of them, and of his two new children. But he had not forgiven the Mexicans for what they had done to his first family. Following the murders, he and many other Apaches had vowed to wage war forever on Mexico. They began their raids again, despite Mangas Coloradas's treaty.

Like birds of prey they swept down on Mexican towns, robbing citizens, stealing horses and mules. The Apaches had developed a taste for mule meat, and they captured lots of mules from the Mexicans. Then on one raid they captured some cattle and ate their first beef. They all agreed that beef tasted much better than mule meat, and they decided to get more.

Geronimo led many of these raids. From time to time Mexican troops struck back. On one such occasion Geronimo's

Marianette, one of Geronimo's later wives

third wife, Nana-tha-thtith, and one of his children were killed.

Still he did not give up fighting. These new killings only fueled his hatred and his passion for victory. In one battle Geronimo was hit twice by bullets. One glanced across his face, just missing an eye, and the other caught him in the side. He spent a long while recovering, but he still believed in the Voice that had said bullets would not kill him. He relished victory in battle, just as he had relished victory in games as a child. Meanwhile, his fellow warriors looked upon him as a figure of even greater power and mystery.

In 1856, word reached Geronimo and the Chiricahuas, with whom he was staying at the time, that a new Indian superintendent wanted to talk with them. This man, Michael Steck, had already visited the Mimbreno and Warm Springs bands, as well as the Mescalero Apaches, a separate tribe that lived farther east. These Indians reported that Steck was a good man. He had given them many presents and promised to draw up boundaries that guaranteed homelands for the Apache tribes. The Apaches thought this had already been done in the earlier treaty, but they said they were happy to go along with his plans.

In the dead of winter Steck traveled to Apache Pass, a great pass through the mountains in the heart of Chiricahua country. There he met with Cochise and the other Chiricahua leaders, including Geronimo. Cochise was one of the most famous Indians in the country, and Steck showed him great respect, telling him it was a high honor to meet such a powerful and renowned chief. Cochise seemed pleased by this. The Apaches didn't have a peace pipe, like some other Indians, but they did smoke often. As a sign of friendship Steck and the leaders sat together and smoked Apache cigars made of tobacco rolled in oak leaves.

Steck gave out presents of beads and clothing to the warriors and said that he wanted good relations with all of the

Apache tribes. Cochise's eyes looked older now but were as keen and intelligent as ever. He promised that the Chiricahuas would be the friends of the Americans.

Steck was particularly anxious to ensure good relations with the Chiricahuas because of the Gila Trail. This wagon route westward to California, used by American settlers and the mail coaches, ran right through Apache Pass. Cochise understood Steck's concern before he had even voiced it, and made a solemn promise that his Chiricahuas would protect the pass and all coaches. These mountains were the ancient homeland of the Chiricahuas, and they loved them as much as life itself; but they were willing to allow others to pass through.

Steck was pleased to hear this. It was important to get the Chiricahuas' aid. But to him this was merely a temporary situation. The American government had a plan the Indians did not know about yet. It wanted to remove all the Apache tribes from their homelands and place them in one reservation, where they could be guarded. Then the Americans would have the use of the lands without having to worry about Apache raids.

Steck did not tell the Indians about this plan. He was too smart for that. He knew that if he did he would not leave Apache Pass alive.

Cochise watched Steck's party head north through the pass at the conclusion of the meeting. He felt content. These Americans were so different from the Mexicans, he thought. These were people the Apaches could trust. Like Mangas Coloradas, Cochise was still inexperienced in dealing with Americans.

A Peace Mission Fails

The town of Pinos Altos, New Mexico, was tiny, but it was booming. Gold had been discovered in the mountains above the town in 1859. No sooner did the word get around the Southwest than dozens of rough, grizzled, ready-for-anything miners began pouring in. Crude wooden buildings were thrown together to house the new population. A general store opened its doors. In time a doctor even took up residence. And, of course, a saloon was built.

The miners were tough and fearless men who had spent much of their lives digging the hard earth in search of precious veins of gold. Many of them had first gotten "gold fever" and traveled to California during the California Gold Rush of 1849. They had spent the years since then panning streams for tiny sparkling gold nuggets, hoping against hope for a big strike. Over time, they had become like gamblers, greedy and hopeful, but rarely winning.

As the strikes became less common in California, miners and prospectors moved back eastward. They returned to the vast, empty lands they had originally passed through on their way to California. As they traveled, their practiced eyes would scan the bluffs, crags, and streambeds for the telltale yellow glint that would make them rich.

Eventually, they would find a strike of gold or silver and settle into towns with names like Esmerelda, Nevada, and Cripple Creek, Colorado. Most of these strikes were small, so the towns remained tiny or died out and became ghost towns. But a few, like Boulder, Colorado, and Tucson, Arizona, prospered from the gold strikes in the region. Over the years these rough-and-ready little towns grew into large cities.

Most of the miners were lawless loners who weren't used to town life. They were more at home sleeping under the stars than in a poster bed with sheets and a pillow. They liked gambling and drinking. They cared very little for the law and order that more civilized communities lived by.

So they never gave a thought to the fact that they had built their town on land that had been granted to the Apaches. Pinos Altos was smack in the middle of Mimbreno Apache country— the homeland of Mangas Coloradas himself. As soon as the miners moved in they started pushing Apaches out. Any Mimbrenos who strayed too near the new town in search of antelope or jackrabbit were greeted by rifle fire. The miners thought they knew all about the wild, uncivilized ways of the Apaches, and they were ready to put down trouble before it began.

Killing Apaches was like a sport for the most lawless of these men. They would sit with glasses of rye whisky in the

Gold prospector in 1850

saloon, boasting about how many Apaches they had shot in the past week or month. The U.S. Army was under orders to protect the Apaches. The treaty with the Indians stated that the Americans would guarantee their protection. But the officers in charge found it impossible to keep an eye on all the miners.

At first the Mimbrenos didn't mind the miners working on their land. They themselves had no use for the yellow stone that made the white men drunk with happiness. But they certainly weren't going to allow themselves to be shot at. The Apaches were, first and foremost, warriors. If they were attacked they would respond with terrible force.

This was exactly what some of the Apaches now wished to do. Geronimo was in Mimbreno country at the time, and he counciled for war. Many of the Warm Springs Apaches were here too. Their two chiefs, Victorio and Loco, were both brave and fierce warriors. Victorio especially—with his wild, flowing hair and eyes that gleamed at the thought of battle—had a passion for warfare and a great distrust of all outsiders, be they Mexicans or Americans. Both of these chiefs joined Geronimo in urging Mangas Coloradas to call for an attack on the miners.

But wise old Mangas Coloradas understood that the problem was not that the Americans were going back on their agreement. It was, rather, that these miners didn't understand that the Apaches had a right to live on this land, and that they had no desire to harm the miners. He decided, therefore, that the decent course of action was to meet with the miners himself and explain the Indians' position.

Geronimo, Loco, and Victorio shook their heads and waved their hands in protest. It was foolish for Mangas Coloradas to expose himself to the miners. They were crazy men who shot at Indians for no reason. But Mangas Coloradas stood firm. White men are not animals, he told them as he mounted his horse. He,

Mangas Coloradas, would explain the Apaches' position. Then, he said, the Apaches would have peace.

* * *

It was a blazing hot summer day in Pinos Altos. The desert winds were whipping up a cloud of dust so thick that one couldn't even see the buildings across the town's one narrow street. The houses were silent. The only sounds, except for the whipping of the wind, came from the saloon. There, a dozen or so miners sat around small tables, playing cards and drinking whisky.

The harsh summer heat made mining dangerous work, and it was always a topic of conversation. Dust filled a man's nostrils and lungs, choking him and making breathing difficult. Everyday someone passed out from heat exhaustion.

Another constant problem was getting decent food. Being so far from civilization it was hard to get supplies. The miners needed fresh vegetables and fruits, and they couldn't rely on supply wagons to get through on the Gila Trail. They had solved this problem by planting gardens and hiring Mexican workers to tend them. This, however, had an unexpected consequence. When the Apaches learned that Mexicans were living and working on *their* land, they refused to stand for it. Apache raiding parties swept down on the Mexicans, whom the Indians considered invaders, and killed several.

This, in turn, angered the miners. It just showed, they told one another, that the Apaches were blood-crazed savages. Why on earth should the Indians want to kill gardeners, who hadn't harmed them at all? And besides, the miners said, the Mexicans were working on *our* land. This incident increased the anger on both sides. It was now a favorite topic of the miners when they discussed the Indian problem.

A table of men in the saloon had gotten themselves worked up on this subject. One of them was a grizzly old fellow with a huge scar down one side of his face and an empty socket where an eye had been (the work, he said, of Sioux Indians in the Black Hills of the Dakotas). He declared that the miners ought to be their own peacekeepers. And the best way to keep peace with the Apaches, he said, was to ride out, hunt down their villages, and destroy every last one of them.

The others at the table agreed that that would be the best solution. The problem, though, was that they were so hard to locate. Whole tribes of them could move in an instant and with no more sound than a gust of wind makes. No, they would have to pick off the Indians one at a time, when they came within shooting range of the town.

At that moment a young man burst through the swinging saloon doors and shouted that an Indian was coming right toward the town. The others thought it must be another raiding party out to kill their Mexican workers. But the young man said no: This was one single Indian—the largest Indian he'd ever seen—riding with no weapons.

Instantly, the saloon emptied. The men poured into the street and hurried to the edge of town. The lone Indian was just visible through the whipping dust. Within a few moments he was among them, and they saw that he was indeed an enormous man who rode tall and erect. He was also very old. His leathery face, lined with deep wrinkles, was like the rough pattern of peaks and valleys that formed his tribe's homeland. Long gray hair flowed down on his shoulders.

The Indian sat erect and noble on his horse amid the swarm of dirty and unkempt miners who had gathered around him. Politely, he asked to speak to their chief. At this there was a great deal of laughter. He said that he was Mangas Coloradas,

Chief of the Mimbrenos, War Chief of the Apaches. The laughter died. Every American in the Southwest knew the name of Mangas Coloradas. With a mixture of awe and hatred they asked what he wanted.

Looking straight ahead and at no one of the miners, Mangas Coloradas said he had come to make peace, to explain that the Apaches wished the miners no harm. The two groups, he said, could live together.

One of the miners, whose eyes were glazed from whisky, said they weren't interested in talking with any Indian while he sat on his horse. Why didn't the great chief come down and talk?

Mangas Coloradas nodded. He said it was proper among his people that men look eye to eye when they speak of important things. He dismounted. As he did the group pushed closer around him. He stood half a head over them, gazing sternly off into the distance, waiting for them to select a leader.

But instead, one of the miners, the one-eyed old man, pointed to the chief's leather jacket. That, he told the others, was white man's clothing. His one eye swept the faces of his friends. This Indian, he hollered, had come in peace while wearing

Wolverine

50

clothing stolen from the white men he had murdered. This, he said, was the way the Indians worked. Making a bargain with them made no more sense than making a bargain with a mountain lion. Indians, he said, understand only violence. He pointed to the ruined side of his face as evidence.

Voices rumbled in agreement, but at the same moment Mangas Coloradas held up his huge palm and instantly there was silence. The Apaches, he said, were men, not animals. They wanted peace as much as the white men. They wanted the freedom to hunt deer and antelope without being shot at by others. And, he said, the Apaches were willing to allow the miners to remain on Apache land.

At this the miners rose up angrily. *Apache* land? This was the miners' town! Mangas Coloradas tried to explain about the treaty he had signed, in which the American government had declared this to be the homeland of the Mimbreno Apaches, but nobody was listening. They were shouting among themselves now, many crying out for an attack on the Apaches to put them in their place.

Then the one-eyed miner grabbed Mangas Coloradas's collar and reminded them of the white men, women, and children the Apaches had killed. Here was their great chief, wearing the clothes of murdered Americans!

In a rush the miners grabbed Mangas Coloradas and pulled him to a nearby tree. Some were for killing him here and now. Others said that if they left some life in him he would return to his tribe and be a warning to stay away from the town of Pinos Altos. They tied the old warrior to the trunk of the tree and began beating him across the back with a bullwhip. All the miners wanted a turn. When one got tired, another took the whip and vented his hatred of the Apaches on the back of their leader. In a frenzy, with grunts of satisfaction, they cracked the heavy whip across the broad, powerful back. Sweat poured from them as they worked. The sun dropped lower in the sky, lengthening the shadows, and still they flailed the man.

At last, when the dusty winds of midday had calmed, the miners were satisfied. They cut the old Indian from the tree and left him in the dirt. No one even checked to see if he was still alive. He had long since lost consciousness.

But life did still beat in the tough old man's body. Lying on his stomach, his back a raw, blood-caked mass of flesh, Mangas Coloradas still lived. As darkness came on, his eyelids fluttered, then opened. His voice was gone, but as his eyes gazed into the sky his cracked lips formed one word: *revenge*!

8

The Apaches Attack

Mangas Coloradas managed to drag himself to the outskirts of the town that night. Several of his warriors, including Geronimo and Victorio, were nervous that he had been gone so long. They crept close to the town in the darkness to try to see what was happening. A party of them came upon their great leader lying unconscious in the dirt and nearly dead. Without making a sound they carried him several miles to where their horses were tied, carefully laid him across the back of a horse, and rode off into the mountains for home.

It took a long time for Mangas Coloradas's injuries to heal, but he did not waste those weeks. He sent his chiefs out to gather the Apaches. Geronimo rode to the Bedonkohes, Loco to the Warm Springs, and Victorio to Cochise and the Chiricahuas. While waiting for the warriors to assemble, Mangas Coloradas pondered the terrible wrong the miners had done to him. He himself had led raids, had killed many men, had tortured men to get them to talk. All of this was the work of a war leader. But he had thought that all men—Indians, Mexicans, or Americans—would respect an unarmed messenger on a peace mission. Now he understood that the miners had not considered him a messenger because to them the Apaches were nothing more than animals.

In late September of that year, 1860, the tribes assembled in a canyon in the Big Burro Mountains, just east of the town of Pinos Altos. First Geronimo, then Mangas Coloradas, and finally Victorio of the Warm Springs told of the inhuman treatment the miners had shown to their leader. Geronimo, respected as a great warrior and as one who had the Power, spoke in a blunt, earthy manner, saying that it was right for Apaches to claim revenge. Mangas Coloradas talked with cold logic: A terrible crime had been committed against one who sought peace, he said. Now they must punish the criminals. Victorio, the fiercest of the Apache leaders, stirred the warriors into a frenzy with fiery cries for blood.

With that the warriors assembled on their horses, bows and rifles on their backs, warpaint across their cheeks. Mangas Coloradas gave a cry, and, like a flash of lightning, the army streaked up the hillside toward the town. Their horses' hooves made thunder in the valley below. For the first time, Apaches were warring on Americans.

They swept down on Pinos Altos and neighboring mining towns. Their attacks were well planned. One body of warriors distracted the miners, who took up positions with their rifles and opened fire. A second body, meanwhile, crept around on foot to the corrals and captured all the horses. Then they rounded up the miners' cattle and sheep, and headed off into the hills.

The main body of attackers continued to fight, using the traditional Apache war plan. From behind rocks and trees they fired careful shots into the miners' settlement, then they silently shifted positions and waited. Eventually, some of the miners would creep out into the open, thinking the Indians had gone. Then a volley of arrows and bullets would fly, striking the miners, who suffered terrible losses.

In time the miners fought back, attacking with ferocious intensity. They got new horses from the Mexicans and went in search of the Apache settlements. They found wickiup settlements and rode through, burning everything that would burn and shooting all that moved. Whole Apache families were slaughtered. Some of these miners had fought Indians in other parts of the West. They now began doing something that Indian tribes other than the Apaches practiced: scalping.

Americans, Mexicans, and Apaches fell by the dozens in the war led by the Mimbrenos. In time, as all parties became weary of combat, the fighting lessened. Many of the warriors of other bands, satisfied that they had avenged their leader, returned home. It looked like the war between the Apaches and the Americans might end in Mimbreno country.

But then something happened farther west at Apache Pass, in Chiricahua country. There, once again, white men would wrong an Apache leader.

* * *

Cochise and his warriors returned home. He had helped the Mimbrenos in their war, but Cochise did not believe he was fighting against all Americans, only against the lawless miners who had wronged the Indians. Cochise still carried out his promise to Superintendent Steck to keep watch over the Gila Trail. He made sure that no harm came to the wagons and stagecoaches. In fact, he had made a business deal with the station manager at Apache Pass. His Chiricahuas provided the station with firewood, and in return the manager furnished him with supplies from the wagons that came through. Cochise still believed that most white men could be trusted.

Shortly after the Chiricahuas had returned home, Cochise received a message from the station manager to come and talk. Cochise thought there might be a new wagon at the station with supplies for him to choose from. He brought his wife and son with him, as well as his brother and two of his nephews.

When the Indians arrived they noticed that a group of American soldiers was camped at the station. It was the leader of the troops, a Lieutenant Bascom, who wanted to speak with the Indian chief. Innocently, Cochise followed the man into his tent.

Once inside Bascom turned on the Indian and began shouting accusations at him. Cochise was confused and couldn't understand what the man was talking about. It seemed that a boy had been taken by raiding Indians from the ranch where he and his family lived near the Chiricahua homeland. These American soldiers were here to get him back, and Lieutenant Bascom accused Cochise of kidnapping the child.

Cochise knew nothing of this matter, nor did any of the Chiricahuas. As it turned out, a group of White Mountain Apaches, who lived far to the north, had captured the boy, but that fact wouldn't become known for many years.

Lieutenant Bascom was a young, inexperienced officer. He didn't know what older officers in the Southwest knew—that Apache chiefs had great honesty and integrity. Bascom's idea of

Cochise

the Apaches came from the newspapers, which portrayed them as insane, bloodthirsty, and utterly untrustworthy.

Bascom refused to believe that Cochise could be telling him the truth. He insisted that the Indians release the boy. Cochise gave him his word that he knew nothing of the affair, but he would send his scouts out to other tribes to find out about it. Cochise told the lieutenant of his long association with Americans and how he guarded Apache Pass. Surely, he could be trusted.

But Bascom wasn't listening. He called his attendants into the tent. One held a gun on Cochise. Bascom said that he would keep Cochise as a prisoner until the boy was returned.

The Indian leader's face lit up with rage. This man didn't believe him! What's more, he proposed to hold him, Cochise, Chief of the Chiricahuas, hostage!

The next thing the soldiers knew, they were standing alone in the tent, and a gaping hole flapped in its side. In one swift move Cochise had whipped out his knife, slashed through the tent, and fled.

Running outside, Bascom ordered his men to open fire on the escaping Indian. One bullet struck Cochise, but it didn't take him down. He leaped onto a horse and sped down the trail, thinking about the members of his family whom Bascom still held. Suddenly, he saw a stagecoach coming up the trail. Pulling his horse into the bushes, he waited until it was even with him. Then he dashed out, flew at the driver, took his gun, and turned the coach around.

There were three men in the coach, men whom Cochise knew and was friendly with because they worked at the station. Nevertheless, he kept them as prisoners. He sent the driver back to Bascom, offering to trade. To his surprise, Bascom refused. He wanted the boy, and he would keep these hostages until he got him.

A few days later Cochise's scouts reported that a large group of army reinforcements had gone to the aid of the troops at Apache Pass. It was quite clear to the chief that the Americans were massing for an attack. So Cochise, as swift and ruthless as a general could be in wartime, immediately ordered his hostages executed. Their bodies were hacked up, then taken to the military post. Cochise wanted his enemy to see the ferociousness of the Apaches, to understand what a terrible thing it was to make enemies of them.

In response, Bascom executed Cochise's brother and nephews.

Cochise's anger was now aroused to a passionate fury by the killing of his kinsmen. He swiftly summoned his warriors to the attack. Over the next two months hordes of Apaches swept down from the surrounding mountain peaks into the camp in the narrow pass. In that time, 150 Americans were killed.

Geronimo was among the attacking Indians. Before the trouble had started, he had led a band of the Bedonkohes to the Chiricahua homeland. He had come to marry one of Cochise's relatives, a young girl named Shega. His own anger at the Americans had been growing steadily. The whipping of Mangas Coloradas proved to him that the Americans could be as treacherous as the Mexicans. Now an official of the American army had shown that the country's leaders were not to be trusted either. He, too, was eager for battle.

Cochise sent Geronimo and his Bedonkohes on special runs to attack the stagecoaches that came through Apache Pass. Geronimo's men hounded the coaches and wagon trains mercilessly, sweeping down on them with their great war whoops, sending arrows into the hearts of the drivers and shotgun riders. They looted the supplies and set the wagons aflame, then vanished into the hills. Soon the word was out all along the Gila Trail, from Texas into California, that venturing into Apache Pass meant certain death. The word "Apache," long feared by Americans, took on an even greater sense of horror.

The great escape of Cochise from the Americans became a legend among the Apaches, who called it the "Slash-Through-the-Tent" escape. But the affair didn't help Cochise to free his family, and it didn't ease his anger at being accused of lying. It did, however, make him understand once and for all that the Americans would never treat the Indians as men to negotiate with, but more like troublesome insects to squash.

On the other side, Lieutenant Bascom didn't realize that he was setting off an explosion of Apache hatred that would continue for twenty-five years. The brutal and intense fighting of that period would be known as the Apache Wars. It would be one of the last—and greatest—struggles for freedom by the American Indians from the white men who were taking over the continent.

As Geronimo said in his simple way: "After this trouble all of the Indians agreed not to be friendly with the white men anymore."

9

"The Greatest Wrong Ever Done to the Indians"

The year was 1861. Lieutenant Bascom and his soldiers were busy fighting Apaches in the hot mountains of New Mexico. To the east their comrades had another problem to deal with: The Civil War had begun.

During the past decade troubles between the northern and southern states had been growing over the question of slavery. Slavery was now illegal in the North, and many Northerners wanted to end it altogether, or at least restrict it throughout the country. Southerners, however, needed slave labor to operate their plantations, so they argued with all their might in support of it.

Back in 1848, after the United States won the Mexican War, an enormous amount of land—including the Apache homelands—was added to the country. This additional land made the slavery argument more heated. The main question was: Would the United States allow slavery to exist in the new territories?

The great men of the day debated the question, including two fiery senators: Daniel Webster and John Calhoun. As the decade wore on, the two sides became more and more bitter. One court case caught everyone's attention. A black slave named Dred Scott went to court to try to get his freedom. His lawyers argued that Scott should be free because his master had moved with him into Illinois, where slavery was illegal. The case went all the way to the Supreme Court, which decided that Scott must remain a slave. The justices said that Scott had no rights under United States law because black people were not citizens of the country.

The North was in an uproar. Newspapers charged that the Supreme Court, by considering blacks to be property rather than people, had rejected their basic human rights.

By the end of the 1850s, when the debate over slavery was at its peak, two other prominent men led the opposing sides. One was Stephen Douglas, a senator from Illinois and an old-time politician who argued in favor of keeping slavery in some parts of the country. His opponent was a little-known lawyer and one-time rail-splitter named Abraham Lincoln. Lincoln, standing tall and lanky in front of enthusiastic crowds, argued that the nation could not hold together much longer with its regions holding such different beliefs. "A house divided against itself cannot stand!" he cried to the crowds.

By 1861, Lincoln was president. The Republican Party, which many Southerners believed wanted to end slavery altogether, was in power. On the heels of Lincoln's election, the state of South Carolina took the amazing step of seceding from the nation. Then, on April 12 of that same year, rebel forces in

South Carolina sent cannonballs crashing in on Fort Sumter, which held forces loyal to the United States. The rebels surrendered, but the battle woke up the North like a gust of cold air. This meant war!

Quickly then, ten other southern states seceded, joining South Carolina. They formed a new nation called the Confederate States of America. The remaining states of the North were known as the Union. Four bloody years of war, in which Americans would fight Americans, had begun.

* * *

The Civil War seemed like a lucky break for the Apaches, who were gearing up for their own war against the Americans. Because of the fighting in the East, most of the troops in Apache territory had to be removed. This left the settlers, most of them miners, to fend for themselves. The raiding Apaches, stripped and painted for battle, attacked towns with a terrible fury, burning houses, killing settlers, and rounding up the livestock for

themselves. The Apaches' ammunition ran out in a short time, but they had deadly accuracy with arrows.

By now Mangas Coloradas and his Mimbrenos had joined Cochise and the Chiricahuas. Together they attacked every coach and wagon that attempted to come through Apache Pass. The traffic on the Gila Trail slowed to a trickle, then stopped. Soon the only passage across the continent was the northern Oregon Trail.

Then the Mimbrenos led an all-out attack on the town of Pinos Altos. The fiesty miners refused to be driven off and a vicious battle took place. But the Indians were too powerful, and there were no soldiers to back up the townspeople, most of whom were killed in an all-day battle. The survivors fled, leaving all their possessions behind. Mangas Coloradas smiled grimly as he entered the town for the second time. He had had his revenge on the men who had so cruelly whipped him.

For a few days after this, a peaceful stillness hung over the gravelly plains and wooded valleys of Apache country. The Apaches retreated to their makeshift mountain lairs and celebrated. They had triumphed over the white invaders, driven them in terror from the Apache homeland. They told each other that the arrogant Americans—settlers and soldiers alike—had fled forever in the face of Apache bravery.

But Cochise knew better. And soon word came from outlying scouts that an enormous force of white men had marched into the town of Mesilla on the Rio Grande, south of Mimbreno country. The odd thing was, these troops were dressed in gray uniforms, not blue. But whether in gray or blue, they were still white men, and Cochise was determined to fight any and all of them to the death.

The Indians didn't know that these were Confederate soldiers. Colonel John Baylor, at the head of a frightful force of

Texas soldiers, was storming northward. Cochise didn't know of Colonel Baylor or of his famous hatred of Indians. And he didn't know that Colonel Baylor had sent the following order to all his men in the region:

> *"The Congress of the Confederate States has passed a law declaring extermination to all hostile Indians. You will therefore use all means to persuade the Apaches or any tribe to come in for the purpose of making peace, and when you get them together kill all the grown Indians and take the children prisoners and sell them to defray the expense of killing the Indians."*

This was a lie. The Confederate government had never passed such a law. Baylor had simply written what he wished his new government would order. Acting on his orders, Confederate soldiers sent messengers to the Apaches saying that they sought peace, and that if the Apache warriors would come into the fort to talk, their safety would be guaranteed.

But the Apaches had grown wise to the white men's false promises. Their answer to the messengers was a hail of arrows.

Not long after they had come, Colonel Baylor and his gray-coated soldiers were themselves forced out of the territory by a group of 2,000 Union soldiers. This troop from California was led by the famous General James Carleton. To the Apaches, one group of American soldiers was the same as another. Their scouts reported that this was the largest detachment yet. The chiefs thought that if they could destroy such a force perhaps the Americans would give up their efforts to steal the land from the Apaches. Cochise and Mangas Coloradas hurriedly set about laying a trap for them.

The site they chose was Apache Pass itself. They knew that the soldiers would have to come through the pass, and that they would have to fill their canteens at the bubbling spring just above the abandoned stagecoach station. Mangas Coloradas placed his warriors amid the high mountain crags overlooking the pass, just out of sight. The Union soldiers were strung out in several companies over many miles. The first one to come through was made up of 300 soldiers, under the command of Captain Thomas Roberts. When all the men were in the pass and heading for the spring, Mangas Coloradas gave the signal. For one second the soldiers heard what they thought must be a thousand whispering insects. In the next second they were clutching themselves as the deadly arrows sunk deep into their flesh.

The soldiers tried to group themselves for battle, but the narrow road through the pass kept them in a line. Then the Apaches who were armed with rifles opened fire. "Retreat!" came the cry from Captain Roberts, and the troops fled back out of the pass.

Mangas Coloradas

Mangas Coloradas kept his men from dashing after the soldiers, for he knew that trained soldiers would regroup and attack again. He preferred that his men fight from concealed perches rather than meet the enemy in the open. His warriors whooped in delight as they waited. Cochise, nervously waiting for the second attack, gave a cry for silence. Then there were no sounds but the buzzing of bees in the summer air and the groans of the wounded soldiers lying below.

Soon the Union soldiers headed into the pass once again, with two enormous covered wagons behind them. Again Mangas Coloradas gave the order to attack and again the air was filled with arrows. This time, however, the troops fired one round at the Indians and dashed for cover. The wagons rolled up. Their covers were withdrawn, and two huge cannons hidden inside blasted at the Apaches above. Smoke and cries filled the air. Warriors lay in pools of blood. The cannons were reloaded and again came the deafening blasts, the black smoke, and the agony. Terrified, the Apaches retreated.

The soldiers immediately charged in and took control of the spring. Captain Roberts then sent six soldiers on fast horses back to warn General Carleton of the danger. Mangas Coloradas, from his perch high above, saw the men take off and guessed their mission. If the Apaches were to regroup and destroy the troops, he knew he could not allow these soldiers to get reinforcements. Immediately, he himself set off after the six messengers with fifty warriors.

They caught up with the six in no time, and a short, vicious fight on horseback followed. One of the riders hit the ground when his horse was shot, and the Indians galloped around to kill him before going after the others. This man, a Private John Teal, realized that he was surrounded by fifty fiercely whooping Apaches and decided that since he was going to die he might as well kill as many Indians as he could first. Using his dead horse for cover, he took aim at one Indian, an unusually large man with flowing gray hair, and fired. The Indian fell. Private Teal started to shoot at the others, but to his amazement they stopped the attack and gathered round the fallen giant. Collecting him on the back of a horse, they turned and quickly headed back into their mountains. Private Teal survived the attack.

Of course, the Indian he had shot was Mangas Coloradas himself. With their leader fallen, the Apaches called off their attack. Mangas Coloradas had not been killed, but he was near death when Cochise rode into a Mexican town with him the next day. They had come one hundred miles to a famous Mexican doctor whom Cochise knew lived there. Exhausted and covered with sweat and dirt, Cochise leaped off his horse and burst into the doctor's office carrying his leader and friend. There were tears in his eyes.

"Heal him," he whispered hoarsely.

The doctor said he would try, but he frowned as he looked at the injury.

Cochise shook his head. Trying wasn't good enough. "If he dies," the chief told the doctor, his face taut with emotion, "this town dies."

* * *

Several months later, a very old and very tall Indian, wearing a wide-brimmed Mexican sombrero and fringed Mexican leggings, rode into the base camp of the Apaches in the mountains of Mimbreno country. A cry of recognition went up. Hundreds of men, women, and children came running. They gathered around him with tears in their eyes, touching his horse and calling his name.

Mangas Coloradas had returned.

He looked even older than before and he had lost a good deal of weight, but the light of wisdom shone in his eyes. He sat before the fire at night, telling of his weeks of healing. He listened to tales of the battles his Apaches had been fighting in his absence. Cochise, Geronimo, and Victorio had been busy keeping the Americans fearful of the Apaches. Soon, when he was strong, Mangas Coloradas would lead them on the warpath again and they would defeat the bluecoats completely. Cochise and Geronimo began sketching out plans they had made.

But Mangas Coloradas held up a hand to silence them. He shook his head. He had thought much about this while he healed, and he had realized that the white men were simply too strong. The Apaches could stay hidden in the mountains and make occasional attacks, but there were just too many white men and they were too well armed. Eventually, they would kill all the Apaches.

The only answer, he told his people, was peace. They must try once again to make peace with the Americans.

At that, Geronimo jumped up in anger. He cried that it was useless to make agreements with the white men, for they broke agreements whenever they felt like it. Victorio nodded. He reminded their chief of how he himself had been treated by the miners when he went to talk peace.

But Mangas Coloradas was determined to try one last time. He would go himself, he said. He folded his arms. The discussion was over.

* * *

Mangas Coloradas couldn't have chosen a worse time to try to talk peace with the Americans. General Carleton hated Indians as much as the Confederate Baylor had. During the time Mangas Coloradas was healing, Carleton had been rounding up one of the more peaceable Apache tribes, the Mescaleros. He had crammed these Indians into one small, desolate reservation, where they starved, fought one another, and dreamed of freedom. As for the "hostiles"—the Apaches who were still free in the mountains—Carleton ordered his men to kill any they saw, without asking questions. Carleton was tired of this Apache problem. Exterminating the few wild ones who remained in the hills would be the simplest solution.

One afternoon not long after their chief's return, two Apache lookouts came into camp. They said there was a Mexican man below carrying a white truce flag who said some soldiers wanted to talk peace with Mangas Coloradas.

Immediately, the other Apache leaders shook their heads and declared that their chief would not go. But Mangas Coloradas himself decided that he would. Victorio, Geronimo, and Cochise told him again and again that it was a trap. Mangas Coloradas, however, only shrugged. He was an old man, he told them. Why should they want to kill him? If he could somehow arrange peace, that would be good. If not, no harm would be done.

The others insisted on accompanying him, however. They rode to the outskirts of a miner's settlement, where the army leaders were. There, the Mexican said he would bring the old chief on alone. But the others protested. Finally the officers in the camp raised a white truce flag to show that they meant no harm. At this the Apaches reluctantly agreed to let their chief go.

As soon as the Indians were out of sight, Mangas Coloradas was surrounded by bluecoat soldiers. Every soldier was pointing a rifle at the old man's head. As one of them gagged his mouth, Mangas Coloradas stared into his eyes sadly and wearily. The young soldier looked away. This was the great chief's last attempt to help his people. He realized that already, for no apparent reason, it had failed.

General Carleton's officer in charge was another general, named West, who was eager to carry out his boss' orders. He walked up to where Mangas Coloradas stood. The old chief towered over him. Then, satisfied, the general walked over to one of the guards and whispered, "I want him dead or alive by tomorrow morning. Do you understand? *I want him dead.*"

That night, as the ancient warrior huddled on the ground near the fire, his guards tormented him. They tried to get him to strike out at them so that they would have an excuse to kill him. They heated their bayonets in the fire until they were glowing, then pressed them against the old man's feet. He pulled his feet away, curling up in his blanket, but didn't let out a sound. Finally, he had had enough. He could understand the need to torture a man so as to get information, but this seemed like nothing more than a game.

"I am not a toy to be played with!" he cried as he sat up. This was enough of an excuse for the soldiers. Calmly they aimed their rifles and shot the old man dead. Not satisfied, they took out their pistols and continued to shoot away at the body. Then one of the soldiers, who had learned some tricks from other Indians, took out a knife and scalped Mangas Coloradas. Finally, the army surgeon, who had admired the enormous size of the chief's head, hacked it off, boiled away the skin, and sent it to a doctor who studied skulls.

Mangas Coloradas, greatest chief of the fierce Apaches, had been humiliated and killed by his enemies while seeking peace with them.

Meanwhile, Mangas Coloradas's sub-chiefs sat waiting for their friend and leader all through the dark night. In the morning, as they waited near the mining camp, their village was attacked by soldiers acting on General West's orders. The soldiers killed twelve Apaches and decorated their saddles with the dead Indians' scalps.

After several days the band of warriors gave up hoping that their great leader was still alive. They returned home to report the news, and heard of the terrible massacre in the village. Sadness fell over the Apaches. There was no sound, not even crying.

Eventually the leaders met again and discussed what to do. By the firelight of a night ceremony they officially made Geronimo, their most courageous warrior, a chief. In the coming days his bravery would be an example to them as they prepared once again for war. After years of leading warriors into battle, Geronimo was now an official leader of his people. Yet he took no pleasure in the ceremony. He, like all the Apaches gathered around the fire that night, was mulling over the great misfortunes of the tribe.

The misty light of early morning broke over the rough mountaintops of their homeland. The Apaches looked ahead to the new day and wondered what it would hold for them. For as long as any of them could remember Mangas Coloradas had led them. Now their respected and beloved leader was dead. And he had not died in battle, gloriously, but by senseless murder. The killing of Mangas Coloradas was, as Geronimo said, "Perhaps the greatest wrong ever done to the Indians."

Once again the Apaches were forced to seek revenge.

10

Apache Birth and Death

Geronimo stooped in the doorway of a crude, dome-shaped wickiup, squinting to see into the darkness inside. There, on a mat spread out on the dirt floor, lay Ishton, his sister, wife of his old friend Juh. Her face was tight with pain and glistening with sweat. The eyes gazed up pitifully at her brother.

Ishton had had many fine, healthy children, but this birth was a difficult one. The medicine man stood outside the wickiup shaking his head. He had seen such cases before. The woman would not live.

Juh was away to the south leading a raid. Since the death of Mangas Coloradas four years earlier, the Apaches had carried out their promise to make the white men pay for their evil. Juh, Geronimo, Cochise, Victorio, and Loco had led hundreds of raids on towns, military posts, wagon trains, and ranches. Since Juh was away, Geronimo—Ishton's nearest relative—had been sent for to sit with his sister while she died. As he knelt and put his hands on Ishton's swollen belly, his brow suddenly creased with anger. The Apaches' war on the white men had caused much bloodshed since the death of Mangas Coloradas. Many Apaches had died during the past year. And now, it seemed to Geronimo, the unborn were not even getting a chance to live. Was this what the future would hold? Would Apaches be killed even before they had lived? Was this what Usen, the maker of all things, wanted?

Geronimo refused to believe it. He decided that he would try to help Ishton and her unborn child. Geronimo was no medicine man, but he had one gift that might be useful. He had the Power.

Immediately, he left Ishton and headed into the mountains. He took no supplies, though it was winter and the wind in the mountains was icy. Up he went, climbing on foot and, over steep rock faces, on hands and knees . . . just as he had once done after the murder of his family. The going was rougher this time. Geronimo was now a man of forty years. He was no longer a spry young warrior able to jump quickly over jutting rocks. Years of raiding had worn away the lightness of youth. In its place, however, was the great strength that came from a knowledge of the world.

At length he reached a spot with a commanding view on all sides. He was standing on the top of a mountain peak. The sides were sheer rock and fell straight down to canyons far below. Beneath him in the distance were great wooded valleys, thick with bushy juniper trees and tall green cottonwoods. Beyond these were rows and rows of rough, dry desert mountains, stretching into the horizon.

On this peak was a patch of green grass surrounded by a stand of dwarf evergreen oak trees. In the middle of the trees a little spring bubbled up. How strange that on top of a dry, rocky mountain there was this little patch of lively green. Geronimo smiled. Surely this was a place where the Power would come to him.

He stayed for days on the mountaintop, calling on Usen to give Ishton the strength to bear her child. He asked for nothing for himself, only for the life of the woman and her child. But Geronimo knew he was not just praying for his sister but for all Apache mothers and babies. He was praying for the future of his people.

During his time of prayer he kept a fire lit to warm himself against the icy gales that blew across the peak. For food, he caught the gray squirrels that lived on the mountaintop.

Four is the number sacred to Usen. On his fourth day, Geronimo was drifting into sleep from prayer when he suddenly thought he heard something.

"Goyathlay."

He thought he recognized the Voice, its hoarse, whispered sound. "Yes! Yes!" he cried. It had been a long time since anyone had called him by his real name. In his eagerness he blurted out his prayer that Ishton and her child might survive.

"The child will be born and your sister will live," the Voice seemed to whisper. Or was it just the wind blowing? The words seemed to come with the icy wind across the high mountaintop.

Geronimo smiled and closed his eyes, thanking Usen silently.

Then Geronimo thought he heard again the promise made so long ago: "And you, Goyathlay, will never be killed with weapons, but will live to old age."

The next day Geronimo walked into camp, covered in dust and with bleeding cuts on his hands and feet. Women of the

75

band ran to him with the news. Ishton had given birth and she and her son were well. The boy had been named Daklugie, which meant "Forced-His-Way-Through."

Geronimo listened and nodded. Usen had smiled on them. The Apache tribe would continue. There was much death in the Apache world, but now there was the promise of life too. Slowly, Geronimo went to his own wickiup, where he slept deeply and dreamed hopeful dreams of the future.

* * *

But in the great outer world forces were at work that would soon spell more trouble for the scattered bands of Indians in their desert homelands.

Away to the east, in a courthouse in the sleepy village of Appomattox, Virginia, two great generals had met on a spring day in 1865. Their names were Robert E. Lee and Ulysses S. Grant. Lee, Commander of the Confederate Armies, had surrendered to Grant. The Civil War was over.

Buffalo with calf

The war had dragged on for four years. Half a million American men and boys were killed in combat. Nearly every family in the nation had had loved ones killed or their homes destroyed.

The Civil War had changed America in other ways. During the war the nation's inventors and factories had worked at top speed on ingenious new ways to bring victory. Some of the inventions were only useful in war, such as the Gatling gun, the first machine gun, and the ironclad warship. Other inventions would be useful in peacetime. The telegraph had made it possible for army commanders to communicate over vast distances. Thousands of miles of telegraph lines had been strung during the war, and would now be used to unite this vast territory.

The Civil War was the first one which used railroad trains to transport troops and supplies. Bridges were built and miles of track were laid during the war, and with amazing speed. The Union Army Construction Corps could build a 150-foot bridge over a river in just fifteen hours.

After the war Americans began to rely more than ever on railroads. In 1869 the first transcontinental railroad line was completed. People could ride from New York all the way to San Francisco—right through the dangerous, untamed, Indian-filled lands between.

During Geronimo's childhood the West had been a wild, vague place in the minds of Americans. Few ventured onto that frontier. Then the California Gold Rush had changed people's idea of the wilderness. With the prospect of gold, the West seemed like a paradise to many, and hundreds of thousands came to try their luck. At the end of the Civil War, with railroads and telegraph lines criss-crossing the land, the western frontier was suddenly much easier to reach. More and more settlers were coming all the time.

The American settlers and railroad builders saw the Indians as nuisances to be gotten rid of. And they did a good job of getting rid of them too. By this time, the Choctaws, Miamis, Cherokees, Creeks, and many other tribes had had their lands taken and their people locked away on reservations. Long before, the American settlers had completely wiped out eastern tribes, such as the Chesapeakes, Wampanoags, Potomacs, and others. Now tribes farther west, such as the Sioux and Cheyennes, were being corraled like cattle. The white men were having their way.

But there was one tribe in the Southwest that moved so quickly, fought so cleverly, and loved freedom so desperately that the settlers found it impossible to destroy them. The Apaches were constantly at war, but for now they were still free.

However, with the Civil War over the United States government could now send skilled troops and shrewd generals to conquer the hostile Apaches who still hid in mountain dens and struck at towns and stagecoaches with lightning speed. The new president of the United States, Ulysses S. Grant, hero of the Civil War, sent the great warrior General George Crook west to Arizona to crush the hostile Apaches into submission.

General Crook was a tall man with short hair, a long, bushy beard, and cold, beady eyes. He was as eager for Indian blood as Baylor and Carleton had been. However, Crook was cleverer than the other officers who had been sent to try to subdue the Apaches.

Others had used traditional army fighting methods against the Indians. Troops were lined up in orderly columns, hauling heavy wagonloads of supplies and ammunition in the rear, advancing slowly and steadily. General Crook realized that such methods were useless in the deserts and mountains. He made his units smaller and lighter so that they were able to move more quickly across dry, rocky terrain.

Most important of all, he learned how the Apaches lived. To do this, he enlisted into the army some of the wisest members of the Apache tribes that had already been settled on reservations. He gave these men presents and special treatment as important members of the army. From them he slowly learned how the Apaches lived and fought in their harsh climate.

General Crook realized that American soldiers could never defeat the Apaches. Even if he learned everything there was to know about the Apaches, it would be impossible to train his men to understand the land as the Indians did. And his men could never learn to exist in the desert, smelling out water and food, as Apache boys were trained to do. So Crook decided to use Apaches to beat the Apaches.

He trained his Apache scouts to work with his soldiers, then laid his plans for the destruction of all free Apaches. He was certain of victory: "If this entire Indian question be left to

Apache scout

me," he wrote to his commander, "I have not the slightest doubt of my ability to conquer a lasting peace with this Apache race."

General Crook sent word to all free Apaches in the mountains that the United States government ordered them to report to the reservations that had been established for them. He gave them until February 15, 1872, to come in. After that time, he would come after them.

By February 7, none had come in. Crook sent out another warning, and meanwhile prepared his soldiers for a long, hard campaign.

On February 14, the free Apaches still had not come in, and Crook's beady eyes sparkled with the old lust for battle. Eagerly, he made last-minute preparations for war.

That very afternoon, however, a messenger flew into the fort with a letter for the general. President Grant was sending another military man, General Oliver Otis Howard, to try to deal peacefully with the Apaches. General Crook was to cease hostilities and let General Howard take charge of the Indian problems. Crook was furious at being replaced, but he had no choice but to let Howard take over.

General Howard was well known throughout the army, not only for his bravery during the Civil War (in which he had lost his right arm in battle), but also for his deep religious feeling. Most soldiers felt uncomfortable when their commanding officer gave them sermons along with their orders, and they often made fun of Howard. But from the moment the Apaches first met General Howard, they liked him. Apaches, too, mixed religion and warfare. They understood this soft-eyed man with the flowing white beard.

General Howard first met with the Apaches who had come onto the reservations. These included many Warm Springs Apaches. They complained that there was no good water on the

Major-General George Crook

reservation, that it was in a colder place than they were used to, and that there was much disease. General Howard promised to set up a new reservation for them in their beloved Warm Springs territory.

Next he wanted to meet with the greatest of all living Apaches, Cochise. This would be difficult, however. Since the killing of Mangas Coloradas, Cochise had sworn never to trust a white man again, and never to look at one except to kill him. There was one man whom Cochise might listen to, though. His name was Tom Jeffords.

Some years before, Jeffords had been in charge of delivering mail along the Gila Trail in New Mexico and Arizona. At that time the job was nearly impossible, for no sooner did a stagecoach start out than it was attacked by Indians. Fourteen of Jeffords's drivers were killed by Apache arrows.

Jeffords decided to take the matter into his own hands. He traveled alone into the mountains above the trail and slowly worked his way to the canyon that Cochise used as his base. Instantly, Apache lookouts captured him and brought him before their leader. When Cochise asked why he had come alone, Jeffords explained that he wished to make a deal with Cochise. He knew that the chief was a noble man who would not harm one who came in peace. This white man's bravery impressed Cochise. The chief and Jeffords became blood brothers, and from that time on no mail riders were harmed.

Since then, Jeffords was known far and wide as the only white man whom the great chief would trust. Now General Howard went to him for help. With the aid of Jeffords and two Chiricahua Apaches named Chee and Ponce, General Howard traveled 350 miles to Cochise's stronghold. On the way the party stopped for the night at Silver City. There, some miners pulled out their rifles to kill Chee and Ponce. General Howard jumped in front of the guns, protecting the Apaches with his own body.

At last the party entered a deep, narrow pass that led into a gorge overhung with cliffs. Here was the stronghold of the Chiricahuas. Cochise greeted his old friend Jeffords warmly, then looked to the strange white man with one arm. Jeffords explained General Howard's mission, and Chee and Ponce told how the general had stood between them and the guns of miners.

Cochise studied the man's face, then he nodded. He himself was an old man now. His hair had gone all gray and his cheeks sagged. He was eager for peace. The past few years had been extremely hard on his tribe. The Apaches had killed more men than they had lost, but Cochise realized that there were millions of Americans to fight, and only a few thousand Apaches. Now he understood why Mangas Coloradas had tried so hard for peace.

Cochise motioned to his wives and they swiftly brought blankets for the men to sit on and arranged them in a semi-circle. "Will the general explain the object of his visit?" Cochise asked.

General Howard answered, "The Great Father, President Grant, sent me to make peace between you and the white people."

"Nobody wants peace more than I do," said Cochise. He asked the general to stay in camp until an agreement was reached.

General Howard stayed for eleven days and became friendly with all the Apaches in the camp. He learned some of the Apache language, played with Cochise's children, and taught them to write their names. In those eleven days, he learned that the Apaches were honorable, hard-working people who had been wronged by a much larger and more powerful group. Their fine treatment of him made him ashamed of the way his country had treated the Indians. When he finally prepared to go he and Cochise had worked out an agreement. The Chiricahua homeland would be made into a reservation, which would belong to the Apaches forever.

Geronimo escorted General Howard back home, riding on the back of the general's horse. As they rode they talked and became friends. Forever afterwards Geronimo spoke highly of Howard. "If there is any pure, honest white man in the United States army, that man is General Howard," Geronimo said years later. "All the Indians respect him, and even to this day frequently talk of the happy times when General Howard was in command of our Post."

When the party reached the group of soldiers who were camped waiting for the general's return, Howard felt Geronimo shudder against his back. The general had heard all about the treachery of the miners at Pinos Altos and the soldiers who killed Mangas Coloradas, so he understood Geronimo's fear. He reassured him that there was no trick. And there was no trick at that time or at any other. General Howard remained as good as his word.

Unfortunately, the United States government did not. Three years later, in 1874, General Howard was gone and a new group of American officers made their way to the Chiricahua camp, again led by Tom Jeffords. They came to report that the government had decided it was too expensive to operate reservations at both Warm Springs and in Chiricahua country, and so the Chiricahuas would be moved.

But when they filed through the narrow entrance to the camp, the officers discovered that Cochise was very ill, too ill to discuss the new decision, and possibly near death. The officers left, but Jeffords remained at his old friend's side. Cochise was suffering from terrible pains in his stomach and chest. Finally, the pain got so bad that Jeffords decided to make a trip to Fort Bowie, where there was a doctor who might be able to help.

Cochise smiled sadly as his friend prepared to go. "Do you think you will see me alive again?" he asked.

Jeffords stopped and stared at the shriveled, pain-wracked form of his friend. Tears began to fill his eyes. "No," he said, "I do not think I will."

Cochise closed his eyes and kept smiling. He winced suddenly as a pain shot through him, then relaxed. "I think I will die about ten o'clock tomorrow morning," he said calmly.

Jeffords left, and Cochise did indeed die the next morning. At the time he was the most famous of all Apache chiefs, known far and wide among Americans as a source of death, terror, and destruction. He died, however, believing that he had brought peace to his people.

* * *

Cochise was dead and the Chiricahuas were without a guaranteed homeland. Many Indians who were living on reservations were dying of disease and hunger. Those who were strong enough fought with the soldiers who held them captive, or escaped to join those living deep in the mountains. Peaceable General Howard was gone, and General Crook once again eagerly amassed his deadly forces and began small-scale wars on bands of free Apaches. It looked like the freedom-loving Apaches living in the mountains were about to be hunted down and exterminated for good.

Then, on a hot summer morning in August of 1874, a young man named John Clum arrived at the San Carlos Indian Reservation. San Carlos was the largest of the reservations and the one where Apaches lived in the most miserable conditions. Clum was only twenty-two years old and had a smooth, clean-shaven face, gentle features, and wore a fancy leather suit with fringes down the arms and legs. He was the new Indian Superintendent.

The soldiers who patrolled the reservation and the miners who lived and worked nearby laughed at the thought of such a young dandy controlling 700 disease-ridden, bloodthirsty savages. Why, he'd be eaten alive! This would be something to see.

Agent Clum marched into the dingy log cabin that was the reservation headquarters and presented his papers to the army officer in charge. Then he asked the officer to leave, and to take all his men with him. The officer was confused. How did Agent Clum expect to keep order without at least one company of cavalry? Didn't Agent Clum know that the Apaches were ruthless?

Agent Clum silenced the man. He was in charge now and he got his way. The soldiers were withdrawn.

Next Clum called together the chiefs of the different tribes and bands on the reservation for a meeting. With their help, he set up an Indian police force, an Indian court (with the chiefs as judges), as well as Indian-run farms and businesses. Within a remarkably short time the reservation was operating smoothly and most of the Apaches seemed happy.

Like most of the white men Clum thought that the Indians must not be allowed to roam free following their old lifestyle. He believed, however, that by treating them decently they could be taught to function as a "civilized" society. General Crook, meanwhile, stalked around the reservation suspiciously, unwilling to believe that the Indians weren't killing and robbing each other. He disliked Clum's whole approach. However, in 1875 he was transferred to another post in the great northern plains of Nebraska, where he was to help control the Sioux Indians. The future for the Apaches looked brighter.

Unfortunately, at this time the government's Indian Office in Washington, D.C., decided to finally go ahead with the plan that the former Indian agent, Steck, had been working on. The office decided to move all the Apaches from all the reservations scattered over Arizona and New Mexico onto one reservation. They chose Clum's San Carlos Reservation.

Over the next year more and more Indians—most of them eager for peace and a chance for a quiet, decent life—moved onto San Carlos. Apaches from the distant White Mountain and Coyoteros tribes poured in. Within a short time Agent Clum found himself in charge of more than 4,000 Indians. There was not enough food for so many, and the rival tribes soon began to fight.

Then the Indian Office ordered Clum to round up one last group. This would be his most difficult task, for these were the fiercest, proudest, most freedom-loving of all Apaches: the Chiricahuas.

11

Geronimo the Rebel

S wift-footed lookouts slipped soundlessly into the wickiup camp deep in the mountains of Chiricahua country. They hurried to a central fire, around which sat Geronimo, Juh, and the two sons of Cochise, Taza and Naiche. These were the leaders of the free Apaches. With them was Tom Jeffords, their only friend among the white men, now more Apache than American.

With the firelight dancing in their eyes, the excited lookouts gave their report. A large group of cavalry was approaching. With the soldiers were many Apaches from the San Carlos Reservation.

Quickly, the warriors prepared for battle. They stripped to their breechcloths, streaked on their warpaint, and shouldered their weapons. Fresh lookouts were sent. With them went Geronimo, Taza, and

Naiche and his second wife, E-clah-heh

Tom Jeffords. By the time they reached the party of white men, though, there were no longer any soldiers. Only the Apaches from the reservation approached them, with a small, fair-skinned, gentle-featured white man leading them.

This was John Clum. He had come to ask the free Apaches to join the others at the San Carlos Reservation. He had been forced to bring the cavalry soldiers with him, but he had left them in the rear and would not use them. Instead he had brought the Apache police from the reservation, so that they could tell their kin of the life there. There would be no fighting. In the name of peace he asked Taza, the eldest son of Cochise, to lead his people to the reservation.

The Indians, with Jeffords, returned to their camp to smoke oak-leaf cigars and discuss the offer. Taza, Naiche, and Tom Jeffords finally decided that it was best to end the raiding and hiding and go to the reservation. But Geronimo set his strong mouth firmly shut and shook his head. He would not be imprisoned, for he had done nothing wrong. An Apache, he said, lives among the canyons and rivers as a free man. He hunts for food and paints himself for war when he is wronged. This is the life of the Apaches. He, Geronimo, would not be caged like an animal.

At daybreak Clum and his Apache police entered the camp to hear the decision. There they found Taza, Naiche, Jeffords, and several hundred warriors, women, and children preparing to follow them to San Carlos. Clum had everyone counted. He knew the names of all the leaders. When the count was finished, he asked where Geronimo and Juh were. Jeffords said they had left, with many warriors joining them.

Clum turned red with anger. His orders were to bring all the renegade Apaches in. Now he had let one of the most famous escape. He believed that he was truly helping the Apaches and that his reservation was the only place for them. He couldn't understand why these chiefs would want to lead their people into hiding. He could only think that they must be insane not to want the civilized life of the reservation.

Angrily, Clum ordered his Apache police to alert the cavalry to follow the runaways. But Taza shook his head. Geronimo was the cleverest of leaders. By now he and his warriors would be deep in the mountains of Mexico. They were gone.

* * *

For Geronimo and his band of runaways the following months were wild and lawless. Cochise was dead and General Howard was gone. They no longer saw any reason to make peace treaties with the white men. They did as they pleased.

And raiding was what pleased them. It was just like the old days, when as boys Geronimo and Juh joined war-painted parties led by Mangas Coloradas. They swept down on Mexican villages, the great war whoop in their throats and blood on their spears. They rounded up herds of cattle and horses and fled back into their mountains. Then they ventured north into New Mexico, where they sold their stolen horses to ranchers and used the money to buy more guns and bullets. They set up a new home in the mountains near the Warm Springs Reservation, and there they settled down for the winter, well-stocked with beef, arms, and whisky.

The wild warriors became fervently devoted to Geronimo. Through his leadership they now had everything they needed for a good life. They took to streaking their cheeks with white warpaint instead of red. They decided this would be a sign of their devotion to Geronimo. Some of these warriors rode down

From left to right: Yahnozha (Geronimo's brother-in-law), Chappo (Geronimo's son), Fun (Geronimo's second cousin), and Geronimo

to the San Carlos Reservation and told their friends who had gone with Clum about the good times. The reservation Indians listened, and wished they had followed Geronimo.

The raiding life was a very good one, but Geronimo knew it couldn't last. It came to an end one day in July of 1877. On that day Geronimo met some messengers from Clum, who said that the agent would like to talk with him. The messengers were Apaches. They sat and drank *tiswin*—Apache whisky—with the free Indians, and joked and told stories. The next day, Geronimo and his warriors followed them. They were so friendly that Geronimo and Juh believed there was no danger. They even brought their wives and children with them.

Clum and six officers were on the porch of the Warm Springs Reservation headquarters. Geronimo and his followers walked into the wide courtyard in front of the building.

Agent Clum made them stop short when he said, "If you will listen to my words with good ears, no serious harm will be done to you."

Geronimo had thought this was going to be a friendly conversation. Now this Indian agent was threatening to harm them! Geronimo stood tall and proud, his sleek black hair blowing in the wind. He replied: "If you, Agent Clum, are careful what you say, no serious harm will be done to *you*!"

At that Clum gave a shout and a file of soldiers streamed out of the supply house across the yard, each with his thumb on the hammer of his gun. The Apaches were surrounded. Within a few minutes, the soldiers had taken their rifles and bows.

Clum smiled grimly at the sight of Geronimo, the great Apache, known for being slippery as a lizard, caught by such a simple trap. Years later, Clum still remembered vividly that picture of Geronimo:

"He stood erect as a mountain pine, while every outline of his symmetrical form indicated strength and endurance. His abundant ebony locks draped his ample shoulders, his stern features, his keen piercing eye, and his proud and graceful posture combined to create in him the model of an Apache warchief. There he stood, Geronimo the renegade, a form commanding admiration, a name and character dreaded by all. His eyes blazed fiercely under the excitement of the moment and his form quivered with suppressed rage."

Clum then ordered Geronimo and his followers to the corral, where they would be imprisoned. Geronimo didn't move but simply stared straight at his enemy. Suddenly, his hand went to his knife. It was the only weapon he had, and he had almost decided it would be better to die fighting than to give up. An alert sergeant sprang forward, however, and kicked the knife out of his hand. "Click!" went the hammers of a hundred guns, as the soldiers circling the captives prepared to fire.

Then Geronimo breathed a deep and heavy sigh, and nodded, the very same way he had nodded a long time ago when Juh had beaten him in wrestling. Once more he was beaten.

The soldiers clamped the warriors' arms and legs in irons and imprisoned them in the corral, since there was no jail. For John Clum it was the happiest day of his life. He had captured the wildest and most dangerous Indians in the Southwest.

But Clum wasn't content merely to capture these Apaches. He had evidence of dozens of murders and thefts they had committed. He had only to put them on trial, so that he could execute them. After that the white people of Arizona and New Mexico would be forever grateful to him, and the Indians at the reservation would live peacefully. Best of all, the United States government would surely thank him by giving him a more important position and a higher salary. All in all it was a great moment for Agent Clum.

But the moment didn't last long. When Clum returned to San Carlos he found a troop of soldiers there who had orders to inspect and manage the reservation. Clum was furious. That was *his* job! At once he sent an angry telegram to Washington, D.C., boasting that he could take care of all the Apaches in Arizona if the government would let him. The Indian Office responded with a curt, "No thank you."

In a rage Clum quit his job and left the reservation, leaving Geronimo and the others still in chains on the dusty plain in New Mexico. Vowing never to work for the government again, John Clum moved to the small town of Tombstone, Arizona, and started a newspaper there.

The new Indian agent, Henry Hart, faced a lot of problems at San Carlos. When he learned that there was a whole band of

Apaches locked in irons in Warm Springs, he immediately ordered them freed and brought to live at San Carlos.

So Geronimo, Juh, and the other "wild" Apaches escaped trial and death. This was the only time in his life that Geronimo was captured. He went quietly to live on the reservation, but not for long. The fierce, freedom-loving Apache could not be content on the quiet reservation forever. He was soon to lead a desperate escape and become famous throughout the land, thanks to newspaper stories about him. Soon Americans all over the country would read about the wicked, bloodthirsty, crazed Apache named Geronimo. And one newspaperman who would write some of the most hateful stories was John Clum.

* * *

For the time being, though, all the Apache leaders and their followers were at the San Carlos Reservation. But life was so bad that every day their frustration mounted and their hearts became more filled with hate. Victorio, proud chief of the Warm Springs Apaches, had reluctantly agreed to come. Now he was furious because on the reservation his people could not raise enough food to feed themselves. They had to get food rations from the U.S. government. The food was given out at a place twenty miles away, and every man, woman, and child had to walk the twenty miles to get his or her share. Victorio complained that many old people in his clan could not do this. The soldiers only shrugged.

Victorio lost his patience. He was a chief to be obeyed, not an old man to be shrugged off! He and Loco led 300 Warm Springs Indians on a great dash for freedom. Rifles blazing and arrows flying, they sped past the guards and headed for New Mexico.

Victorio

The runaways spent a frigid winter in the high mountains, desperately searching for food and running from soldiers. Finally, Victorio agreed to give up, but he insisted on living at Warm Springs. "Our home is there," he told Captain Bennett, the man who had finally caught up with him. "My people were born there and they love their home. And further, not one of my men will return to San Carlos!"

The army offered another home, the land of the Mescaleros. Exhausted, Victorio agreed to go there. But he remained deeply distrustful of all white men. Then one day not long after his tribe had been relocated, some men in Silver City went to court to charge Victorio with the murders of several ranchers. Victorio was to be brought to trial and, if convicted, he would be executed.

Victorio hadn't even been in the area at the time of the murders. He would probably have been able to win the case. But he wasn't going to try. Tears of frustration and rage burst from the stern-faced warrior. The false charge made him almost insane with anger. The fury and frustration that had been building up inside the proud chief burst out once and for all. He was convinced that the white men were simply using any excuse they could think of to kill him.

Silently, Victorio and his warriors rounded up horses while their women got the children ready to go. On Victorio's signal his warriors stabbed their guards and others brought the horses around. Then once again the Warm Springs Apaches tore off into the mountains. Victorio declared that there would be no more captures, no more peace treaties. This time they would fight to the death.

"I will make war forever on the United States!" Victorio cried to his people once they had made it to their mountain retreat. And the people, feeling utterly betrayed by the white men, cheered him with all their might.

No sooner did Victorio escape than newspaper headlines throughout the Southwest spread the news of Victorio and his terrible exploits. They reported that the runaway Indians and their wild-eyed leader had murdered two sheep herders. They had broken into a cavalry ranch and stolen forty-six horses. They were ranging over the plains, brutally slaughtering citizens. Victorio had indeed gone mad. In his fury at the white men and their two-faced government, he was lashing out at everything that moved.

All troops throughout the Southwest were joined in a great hunt for Victorio. But Victorio was still a skillful general. As the first soldiers to find him began to close in, they suddenly found themselves trapped in a narrow gorge while bullets and arrows rained mercilessly down on them. They were wiped out by the famous Apache ambush.

Next a posse of fifty-two mountain men and trappers thought they had Victorio. But they soon found themselves in the same terrible position. They were trapped in a canyon for ten hours. At the end of the fighting, thirty-two of them lay dead and eighteen were wounded. Only two men emerged unhurt.

A short time later a company of soldiers under Captain Henry Carroll had closed in on Victorio and were preparing to go in for the kill. They came to a cold spring and stopped to drink. They had no Apache scouts with them who could warn them that the water was loaded with gypsum, a poisonous mineral. Instead of moving ahead and attacking the next morning, they all lay on their sides clutching their stomachs. Instead of fleeing, Victorio and his men turned and attacked the helpless soldiers.

Finally, it looked like Victorio was caught. An Indian scout in the service of the army, named Parker, and his seventy-five tough warriors had chased Victorio's party into a canyon. In the fighting they had wounded Victorio. Now they had only to finish them off. But they had to wait until more ammunition came. While they waited, one of the women of Victorio's band came out of the canyon. She, and all the others in the band, now believed with all their hearts that the whole United States had gone crazy and would not be satisfied until everyone could see Victorio's dead body. She, for one, was determined never to let this happen.

"No white man will ever see Victorio's body!" she vowed. "If Victorio dies, then we will eat him!"

But she did not carry out her terrible threat. The ammunition never arrived, Victorio's wound healed, and he and his people escaped once again.

Gradually, large columns of soldiers were working their way south into Mexico. Several American columns closed in on him, and at the same time a Mexican force of 1,000 men reached him. The Mexican government was offering a reward of three thousand dollars to the man who killed Victorio, so the Mexicans were especially eager for the kill.

It was the Mexican forces that finally did the job. By this time there were only about 200 people in Victorio's band, and half of them were women and children. The huge Mexican company surrounded and attacked the band. By now Victorio's men were utterly exhausted and out of ammunition, so the Mexicans had an easy time. They killed seventy-eight Indians, including wild-eyed Victorio.

Newspapers throughout Arizona flashed the headline: "VICTORIO IS DEAD!" Townspeople rejoiced, ranchers breathed a sigh of relief, soldiers took a much-needed rest. Everyone felt that America was rid of one of the most terrifying of Apaches. The white settlers thought they could relax for a while.

But they were wrong. Victorio was not the only Apache who had kept the idea of freedom burning in his heart. One of the few who escaped from the massacre of Victorio's band was an old chief named Nana, who had hated Mexicans and Americans all his life. As the settlers rejoiced, he was busy gathering a new group of warriors.

Then, soon after the news of Victorio's death had put a smile on the faces of settlers, other news came that wiped it away: Geronimo had escaped!

12

"Geronimo" Enters the Vocabulary

While Victorio was terrorizing the Southwest, another encounter between the Indians and white men was taking place far to the north. The Nebraska Territory was a land of rushing streams, rolling grasslands, and crisp, fresh air. In it lived a peaceable, friendly Indian tribe called the Poncas. The Poncas raised horses and grew beans and corn on the banks of their beloved river, the Niobrara. Unlike the Apaches they had never had enemies. They had no quarrels with anyone, white or Indian. When the first Americans came to their lands they had greeted them with smiles and offerings of food.

The Americans, however, wanted more. They wanted the Poncas' land. Their greatest chief, Standing Bear, said that his people would prefer to remain on their land. In response, the soldiers moved in and forced the people from their homes. "The soldiers came to the borders of the village and forced us across the Niobrara to the other side," said an alarmed Standing Bear, "just as one would drive a herd of ponies."

The army drove the whole peaceable tribe on foot across 500 miles to a reservation they had set up. The weather was harsh during the journey, and many of the very old and very young Indians fell sick and died. Even after they reached their new home the Indians did not recover. Not being used to the warmer climate of the south, many more became ill and died. "We thought we should die, and I felt that I should cry," said Standing Bear, "but I remembered that I was a man."

Standing Bear and the other chiefs decided to lead their people back to their old home. Perhaps they would be killed for returning, but if they stayed where they were they would die anyway.

The army sent one of its best Indian fighters after the Poncas. It was none other than old, beady-eyed General George Crook, who had learned the ways of the Apaches in order to beat them, but had been transferred to this part of the country before he could carry out the job.

Rabbit

Crook's men captured the Poncas with no trouble and General Crook himself went to talk with Standing Bear. He was prepared for an angry confrontation with a wild-eyed, hateful Indian.

Instead he found himself standing before a gentle, smooth-skinned man whose eyes shone with peace and sadness. General Crook, the fierce Indian fighter, softened at the sight. Perhaps for the first time in his life, he realized that Indians were human beings. The wildness and lawlessness of the Apaches had made it easier for him to think of them as animals. Crook once called the Chiricahuas "the tigers of the human species." Now this quiet, peaceful man who sat telling him the sad tale of his tribe seemed to touch the old war leader's stone heart.

After the meeting, General Crook decided to help the Poncas in whatever way he could. He arranged for a lawyer to represent the tribe. Their case went to court and, unbelievably, the Poncas won the right to return to their homeland.

When the judge's decision was read, Standing Bear smiled and shook hands with his lawyer. His people cheered. And General Crook, once a sworn Indian hater, sat in the back of the courtroom smiling softly. Standing Bear, the peaceable Indian, had taught him something.

* * *

Three years later, on September 4, 1882, General Crook rode into the army headquarters in Arizona and took charge of it once again. On that very same day, 2,000 miles away in New York City, Thomas Edison flipped a switch and filled the dark vastness of the city's Central Train Station with light. It was the nation's first business to use electricity. As General Crook sat down at his desk, he too was filled with a new light. He had returned to Apache country not to wipe out the hostile Indians, but to listen carefully to their side of the story.

Soon parties of Apaches from the reservations were filing in and out of General Crook's office. He held meetings with them to learn of their problems. The soldiers watched the Indians moving about like important dignitaries and shook their heads. Old Crook must have gone crazy, they thought. Instead of silencing the Indians' complaints with punishment, he was treating them like, well, like people!

General Crook soon learned some startling things. The Apaches' cornfields and melon patches were constantly being destroyed by white settlers who wanted the Indians to continue living on government supplies. These same settlers, it turned out, were the ones who sold the supplies to the government. If the Indians grew all their own food, these men would lose money.

Crook also discovered that settlers in the area were deliberately taunting and teasing the reservation Apaches so that they would turn hostile and flee! There were two reasons for this. First, if the Apaches all turned hostile, the men in Tucson who sold guns to the army would make more money. Second, if the Apaches all left the reservation, the settlers hoped that they could take over the land for themselves.

General Crook was an old man who had been around for a long time and seen many evil things. But he found these crimes shocking. He immediately called in all his officers and began issuing new orders. He also wrote to Washington, D.C. He was determined to put a stop to this wickedness.

But it was too little and too late. It was this wickedness that finally drove Geronimo off of the reservation. Geronimo was now about fifty-five years old, an old man by Indian standards. But although his face was crossed with lines, age had not slowed him down; nor had it dulled his passion for freedom. Every night on the reservation he lay gazing into the darkness while images of his childhood filled his mind. He could see himself as a boy hunting free along mountain streams, helping the adults plant melons, sitting at night by the warmth of the fire while his mother told him the tale of the boy Apache.

Yes, he knew he was old. And yes, he understood that all the Apaches together were only a small group, while the Americans were a great and powerful one. But Geronimo continued to dream of a day when his people could once again live in their own way.

At last, he could stand the captivity and the unfair treatment no more. On a moody September night, with a hot wind whipping up from the south and great thunderclouds gathering in the sky, he, Juh, and Naiche led almost one hundred of their people to the stables. There, silent as could be, they mounted horses, opened the gate, and slipped away.

When the newspapers learned of the escape, they whipped it into a big story. Everyone remembered the terror Victorio had caused. The name Geronimo was not as well known, but thanks to John Clum and other reporters people were now reading about him. The papers said that another Apache chief had risen, one who was even more clever than Victorio, and possibly just as vicious.

Meanwhile, the escaped Apaches were thrilled by the feeling of freedom. They had separated into smaller parties and then galloped with amazing speed into the high Sierra Madre Mountains of Mexico. Gradually, the groups came together at the base of a pine-covered mountain. First the Nednai Apaches arrived, with bearlike Juh leading them. Then Naiche, with many of the Chiricahuas, appeared in camp. They were still waiting for Geronimo's party when who should arrive but wrinkled

Geronimo, 1890s

old Nana. He had escaped from the massacre of Victorio's band, leading a small number of warriors, women, and children. The others cheered the arrival of friends they hadn't seen in a long time.

Then the scouts came to report that Geronimo's party was on the way. Suddenly Juh, feeling more lighthearted than he had in many months, got an idea. "Let's play a joke on him!" he cried. With that, they kicked out their fires. In the twinkling of an eye, they were all hidden behind rocks and trees. The campsite looked deserted.

Geronimo came ahead of his party into the meeting place. He dismounted from his horse and looked cautiously around, his eyes slitted with worry.

Suddenly, old Nana appeared before him as if by magic, a huge, toothless smile on his face. A snicker came from the bushes, then another. Finally, the whole place was filled with laughter.

Geronimo frowned. "I knew all the time you were here!" he cried to the others.

"You did not!" said Nana. "And you the sly fox of the Apaches!"

The whole gathering broke into laughter again. At last Geronimo's serious face softened and a smile appeared. It was one of the few happy moments for the Apaches. Captivity was behind them and sweet freedom lay ahead.

But not all of the Apaches were free. Loco and his people had not escaped with them. Geronimo had not only been restless on the reservation, he had also been worried. The Apaches who stayed there were slowly forgetting their traditional ways, and the youths who were growing up on the reservation had never learned the art of warfare. Geronimo was very worried that the Apaches were growing weak. He decided that Loco's people must be rescued.

So, after much singing, dancing, and feasting, the Apaches prepared to go right back from where they had come. The leaders worked out a plan to free the reservation Indians. It was Ishton, the wife of Juh and sister of Geronimo, who actually thought of the plan. The leaders had long recognized her wisdom and often looked to her for strategy.

Before they left, Geronimo separated from the others and, singing holy songs, fell into a trance. The others watched their leader respectfully as he slowly rose up and began speaking in words they could not understand. The Power had come to him.

When he returned to them he reported that the Voice had told him they would succeed in freeing their friends. Heartened by this good news, the Apaches broke camp and started on the long trek north.

Geronimo's words proved true, for everything worked just as Ishton planned it. They only had to kill two people at the reservation, both of them Apache policemen. In a short time Loco's people were reunited with them, and they were all fleeing back across the Mexican border. A cavalry party set off in pursuit and had nearly ridden them down when the Indians crossed the border. Once in Mexico again the Apaches felt they were safe, since U.S. troops weren't allowed to cross the border. They made camp, and the women set about preparing food while the men sang songs. It was an exciting night, for many of the young children had never known the life of freedom.

Lieutenant George Forsyth, however, was not going to let the border get in his way. He and his men dashed across, and before the Apaches knew what was happening the horses of the attackers had burst among them. Flying to his feet, Geronimo ordered everyone behind a small mound of rocks that stood in the center of the plain. His warriors rushed to their weapons and returned fire. The fighting lasted most of the night, and the Apaches lost fourteen men.

The next day the Apaches slipped away and began heading deeper south. Suddenly, a column of Mexican soldiers appeared and rode straight for them. Now they had Americans behind and Mexicans in front. The Apaches retreated into a deep, dried-up riverbed. The women dug into it for protection while the men made footholes along the sides from which to stand and shoot.

For a while they held off both armies. The Apaches could hear the Mexican commander urging his troops on in Spanish. "Geronimo is in that ditch!" he cried. "Go in and get him!"

Then, to the Apaches' dismay, they saw the American and Mexican commanders meet in the distance. Now, they thought, the two armies would unite to destroy them. But to their surprise the opposite happened. The Mexican commander was angry that the Americans had ventured onto Mexican territory and he insisted that they leave at once. Lieutenant Forsyth had no choice but to obey.

When Geronimo saw the Mexican and American commanders arguing, he proved what a clever general he was. He ordered his warriors to set the grass all around them on fire. The dry scrubs went up in a sudden whoosh of flame, causing both enemy armies to fall back and allowing Geronimo to make a rapid retreat. Within moments the enemy had recovered, but by then it was too late. The wily Apaches had vanished into the landscape, safe once again.

Back at headquarters General Crook shook his head as he heard the details of this escape. He now realized that it was impossible to beat the Apaches in battle. They were too clever

Geronimo's camp, with Apache guard, in the Sierra Madres,
one mile from General Crook's camp

at striking at their enemy and then vanishing. Still he simply couldn't allow them to roam free. Reports came to him every day of raids the runaways were carrying out on ranches throughout Arizona and New Mexico. Peaceful negotiation was the only tool that might work. He decided to try it.

* * *

In the spring of 1883, Crook rode into the narrow gorge in the Mexican mountains that led to the hideaway of Geronimo's rebel Apaches. His troops had not gone far when a soldier gave a cry and pointed to the rocks above. There two sleek Apache warriors sat on their horses, rifles in their hands and a white streak of paint across their faces. They were not here to fight, however, but to ask what the white men wanted.

Crook explained that he wanted to talk with Geronimo. He was told to wait there and set up camp. Soon, to Crook's surprise, the entire army of Apache rebels was among them, unarmed, talking and joking with his Apache scouts.

Geronimo trotted up to the general and dismounted. Together they went into Crook's tent. Geronimo immediately explained his position. He said that the Apaches had escaped because treatment was so unfair on the reservation. He told the general he was sorry for raids they had made, but he explained that they were on the run and being hunted and had no choice but to steal food. He finished by saying that he and all his people would like to settle. They would be willing to live on reservations if they could be sure they would be treated decently.

To Geronimo's surprise General Crook agreed with all his complaints. He apologized for the terrible way the Indians had been treated. He personally would guarantee fair treatment from now on, and would listen to all complaints the Apaches had. The fact was, he explained simply and honestly, with Geronimo's band roaming free, townspeople throughout the territory would continue to be afraid, so troops would keep trying to hunt them down. As a leader, Geronimo must realize that his people would only be safe on the reservation.

Geronimo liked this gruff, honest general, and he understood the wisdom of his words. He gave one short nod. He had agreed.

With that, the Apache renegades once again filed slowly northward and began a settled life on the reservation. Crook kept his word and conditions improved. At first some of the new soldiers assigned to the reservation kept clear of these wild hostile Indians they had heard so much about. But they soon found that the once-hostile Apaches were actually quite friendly when given respect. "In fact," said one soldier, Lieutenant Davis, "we began to find them decidedly human. Much to my surprise, I found that they had a keen sense of humor and were not averse to telling jokes on themselves as well as on others."

Even though things were going well on the reservation, in the surrounding towns people were not happy. Newspapers didn't like the way General Crook had captured the hostile Apaches. They claimed he should have punished them for running off. They even declared that General Crook, the old war hero, was afraid of battle. Not only that, he was afraid of one lone Indian. The real reason Crook had not fought, many charged, was that he was terrified of Geronimo's cunning and power. The situation got tense as citizens took sides, some claiming Crook had done the decent thing while others agreeing with the newspapers that he was a coward.

Leading those who complained about Crook were the arms dealers in Tucson. These powerful men had insisted that the army bring in more soldiers to the area, supposedly to keep the peace. But the real reason the arms dealers wanted more troops was to have a market for their weapons.

The army's move, however, had disastrous results. When the Apaches saw the gathering of troops, their minds flashed back to other times when the U.S. Army had ganged up on them. One night Geronimo and some of the other leaders began talking about the situation. Geronimo didn't like it. The more he thought about it, the more it reminded him of the time Agent Clum had captured him at Warm Springs. He had spent four months in chains then.

Suddenly, he sat up and his chair went flying behind him. The others all jumped up too. They were not going to sit by and be butchered by army troops! No, they would run!

This time the Apaches fled the reservation because of the mistaken belief that the extra troops were there to harm them.

Once again the runaways fled south in the night. Before they left, Geronimo cut the telegraph lines so that the San Carlos soldiers couldn't wire ahead for help.

Geronimo could never have imagined that in slipping out of the reservation, this time at the head of one hundred of his people, he was making himself into a kind of superstar. "THE APACHES ARE OUT!" cried newspapers. For some, only one word was necessary as a headline: "GERONIMO!" The name came to mean something like "Charge!" or "Attack!" or "Here goes!" It signified the terror that settlers in the Southwest felt at the sight of Apaches.

"Geronimo" had become a new word in the American language.

Mountain lion tracks

13
Last Try for Freedom

Immediately, two columns of cavalry dashed southward in pursuit of the escaped Apaches. Soon it was learned, though, that the Indians had escaped across the Mexican border. General Crook ordered most of his troops to spread out along the border and guard against their return. Meanwhile, two special regiments, containing 192 Apache scouts, slipped across the border to track down the runaways. General Crook had long ago learned that the best way to catch Apaches was to use other Apaches.

For both the Apache scouts and the regular troops, the going was incredibly difficult. It was July, and the sun beat down mercilessly on the men as they traveled across parched plains and over high, rocky mountains. Then the rains came. For weeks on end the soldiers hunted their prey through a constant down-pour. "The troops have been almost continually drenched to the skin for the last month," General Crook reported to his headquarters.

What was making the task especially difficult was Geronimo's clever leadership. The wily Apache understood his position. He knew that hundreds of soldiers were following him, and that General Crook's Apache scouts were sure to be hot on the trail of his band. So Geronimo made the trackers' job tougher by splitting his band up into many small parties. They crisscrossed the rough terrain, meeting up at certain spots for a day or two and then separating again.

All were extra careful to cover their tracks. Geronimo made his people march for miles down the middle of stream-beds so that there would be no footprints for the scouts to follow. This meant that the scouts, and the troops who followed them, wasted a lot of time traveling upstream and down to find the trail again.

But if the going was rough for the scouts, it was just as rough for the Indians. Geronimo could sense the dangerous position he had led his people into. He now knew that white people throughout the Southwest were crying out for his capture. He was so well trained in the arts of warfare and hunting that he could sense the size of the force that was pursuing them. This, he knew, was the Apaches' last try for freedom. He had to use all of his wits to outsmart his pursuers.

The other leaders with Geronimo were Mangas, son of Mangas Coloradas, Naiche, son of Cochise, and old Nana. These men, like Geronimo, all sensed the desperate situation not only of their band of runaways, but of all Apaches. Gripping them all was the terrible understanding that the proud Apaches, who had roamed free for centuries, were fast losing their freedom and their way of life. Desperately now, the leaders set about training the young boys in the band to be warriors, just as they themselves had been trained. Whenever there was a day's rest from the pursuers, Geronimo would give each boy a mouthful of water and set them running up and down a mountain, as he had been trained.

But there was little time for such training. The band was constantly being followed. Occasionally, Geronimo would send a party to ambush the scouts. This was a good way to push the scouts farther back, but also after every ambush one or two fewer warriors returned.

To stay alive, the runaways were forced to raid farms and ranches for food. The raids left a trail of death, which only increased the clamor for Geronimo's capture. Soon Mexican troops also were dispatched to bring in or destroy the plundering Apache band.

With both Mexicans and Americans after him, Geronimo realized he could not hold out for long. Soon a party of scouts from the American side caught up with him. Instead of firing on them, Geronimo talked. He told the soldier in charge that he would meet with General Crook. Crook, who was being ridiculed in newspapers for letting the Apaches escape, was anxious to end the chase. He sped down from Fort Bowie, far to the north in Arizona.

In March of that year, 1886, the runaway warriors appeared one by one before the American troops assembled in a shady valley of the Sierra Madres. Geronimo, dressed in a leather jacket and with a bandana around his head, came forth last of all. General Crook and his men took seats on the ground, and Geronimo did likewise. His warriors stood in a ring around the area, on the lookout for a surprise attack.

Geronimo talked long and eloquently. His voice shook with the desperate hope that there might still be a way for his people to return to their way of life. He explained why his

COURTESY SMITHSONIAN INSTITUTION NATIONAL ANTHROPOLOGICAL ARCHIVES

Naiche and Geronimo in 1886

people had fled, and told how they had always wanted nothing but freedom to live in their old ways. He ended by asking General Crook to treat his people fairly: "There is one God looking down on us all," he said. "We are all children of the one God. God is listening to me. The sun, the darkness, the winds, are all listening to what we say now."

General Crook said he would be fair with the Apaches, but there would have to be punishment. They would all be sent away east to Florida, he told Geronimo. There they would remain imprisoned on reservations for two years. Then they could return to reservations in their native land.

Geronimo had no choice but to agree to this. Finally, the great Apache chief surrendered. "Once I moved about like the wind," he said. His face was wrinkled in pain but his eyes were

116

fixed firmly on General Crook. "Now I surrender to you and that is all."

* * *

But that wasn't quite all. Throughout that night and the next day, as the Apaches thought about what they had agreed to, they began to feel more and more nervous. The thought of being moved far away and imprisoned was frightening. As night came on, Geronimo and his companions sat drinking whisky to calm their nerves. They had gotten the whisky from an old troublemaker named Tribolett who made his living this way. While they sat with him he filled their heads with lies. As soon as the army got back across the border, he said, it would execute all the Apaches. He said they were fools to walk into such a trap.

In their drunken state Geronimo and Naiche decided that what Tribolett said must be true. They roused as many of their band as would follow and slipped off into the darkness. There were only forty of them in all, including twenty warriors, and they got away with no problem.

When General Crook returned without Geronimo, his superiors in Washington, D.C., severely criticized him. They said he had become far too gentle in dealing with Indians. President Grover Cleveland himself was angry at the way Crook had handled the Apaches. Crook was furious at not being allowed to explain the situation. He asked to be removed from command of the territory. The War Department immediately honored his request. Within a month there was a new commander.

The new man was Brigadier General Nelson Miles. Like Crook, Miles was an old veteran of many Indian wars. He had battled Sitting Bull and the Sioux to the north in the Black Hills, and the peaceable Nez Perces in the far northwest. Unlike Crook, though, he had never developed any special fondness or

117

respect for the Indians. He believed that a swift, decisive attack was the best way of dealing with troublesome runaways.

As soon as he arrived in Arizona, Miles set off after Geronimo's twenty warriors with an army of five thousand soldiers. General Miles didn't trust Apache scouts so he dismissed them, relying instead on a swift cavalry regiment. His troops fanned out all across Arizona, New Mexico, and northern Mexico, scouring canyons, gulches, and valleys.

Geronimo's little band was in trouble. Not only were they hotly pursued, they were low on supplies. "At one time we had no water for two days and nights and our horses almost died from thirst," he later said. As he pushed his exhausted friends and family members onward, Geronimo became grimmer and hatred set in his heart. Moving through Mexico, he said, "We attacked every Mexican found, even if for no other reason than to kill. We believed they had asked the United States troops to come down to Mexico to fight us.

"We were reckless of our lives," Geronimo went on, "because we felt that every man's hand was against us. If we returned to the reservation we would be put in prison and killed; if we stayed in Mexico they would continue to send soldiers to fight us; so we gave no quarter to anyone and asked no favors."

Eventually, one of Miles's lieutenants, Charles Gatewood, caught up with the desperate Apaches. Gatewood and Geronimo met. Gatewood told the Indians that the rest of the Chiricahua Apaches were no longer on the reservations in Arizona and New Mexico, but had all been sent to Florida. Geronimo's band must surrender to General Miles, Gatewood said. Then they would be sent to join their people.

Geronimo stared long and hard at Gatewood. He then startled the young man by asking a series of questions about General Miles, whom Geronimo had never met. "What is his age?" Geronimo wanted to know. "Is his voice harsh or agreeable? Does he talk much or little? Does he look you in the eyes or not? Has he many friends? Do people believe what he says? Do officers and soldiers like him? Has he had experience with other Indians? Is he cruel or kind-hearted?"

Gatewood, a little confused, answered the questions as best he could. Geronimo listened to all the lieutenant had to say about his general, then said one more startling thing. "Consider yourself one of us and not a white man," Geronimo told Gatewood. "Remember all that has been said today, and as an Apache, what would you advise us to do under the circumstances?"

The aging warrior then squinted and stared hard at the lieutenant. The fate of his small band, the last free Apaches, lay in the young man's answer.

"Trust General Miles and surrender to him," Gatewood said simply.

Geronimo turned and gazed out across the rocky peaks and rolling valleys he had roamed all his life. Then turning back to Gatewood he nodded and folded his arms. For the last time Geronimo had surrendered. There would be no more escapes and no more raiding for the Apaches. And there would be no more freedom.

𝔕𝔕𝔕𝔕𝔕 **14** 𝔕𝔕𝔕𝔕𝔕

Geronimo on Display

A group of Apache women sat around a fire, weaving cloth and making pottery. The men squatted in their own circle closer to a wickiup, carving bows and arrows as they had always done. They all laughed and chatted as they worked. It seemed like a perfect picture of Apache life.

The problem was that it wasn't real. Just beyond the Indians' campsite a rope was stretched. Behind the rope dozens of white people stood on tiptoes to get a better view. Some talked and pointed, others laughed out loud at the stupid, primitive ways of the Indians, and a few watched respectfully. They all knew that this was not a true Apache village, only a model of one. There were no more real Apache villages.

The year was 1904, and this was the "Apache Village" exhibit at the World's Fair in St. Louis, Missouri. The Apache Wars had been over for eighteen years now, and everyone knew that there was nothing more to fear from these once-fierce Indians. Now that the Americans had beaten the Apaches and destroyed their traditions, they were suddenly eager to preserve those traditions in exhibits, museums, and books.

Beside the "Apache Village" exhibit was a booth that was reserved for the old chief of the Apaches. Here Geronimo sat, a wrinkled old Indian in white man's clothes, selling photographs of himself for twenty-five cents. He was allowed to keep ten cents of this, and the rest went to the businessmen who promoted him. He was the most popular exhibit at the fair, and his pictures sold out quickly. The legendary, fearsome warrior had become nothing more than a curiosity.

But Geronimo had not given up the Apache cause. It was now eighteen years since he had surrendered to Lieutenant Gatewood and General Miles. Since that time he and his people had been prisoners. Geronimo didn't mind people gawking and staring at him at the World's Fair, but deep in his heart the wish to be free still burned. He was no longer a war chief, but he was still the spokesman for the Chiricahua Apaches, and he was still angry at General Miles for not giving them a homeland.

For many years the 498 Apaches of the bands who had survived the wars had lived in miserable conditions on reservations in Florida and, later, Alabama. Their numbers steadily decreased. During their first year in Florida, twenty-two died. Twenty-seven of the 112 children died within a short while after their relocation. The cause was tuberculosis. A doctor who finally examined them reported that the Apaches' lungs, so used to the dry climate of their homelands, could not withstand the moisture and humidity of their new home. Geronimo worked

COURTESY SMITHSONIAN INSTITUTION NATIONAL ANTHROPOLOGICAL ARCHIVES

Apache prisoners, including Naiche and Geronimo (center of first row),
on their way to Florida, 1886

tirelessly to get the United States government to grant his people a reservation in a healthy place.

Finally, the Comanche and Kiowa Indians, who were now living on a reservation in Oklahoma, heard of the Apaches' situation and agreed to grant them a portion of their land as a home. The chiefs had scowled at first. They had never been fond of the wild Apaches. But times had changed. They realized that all the Indians must help one another. And besides, they knew what it was to be torn from one's lands, to be without a home.

The new reservation in Oklahoma was a better place than Florida. But it was not the Apaches' home, nor did it have a similar climate. They were still prisoners. In their hearts the Apaches remained bitter.

It wasn't long before shrewd businessmen in the Oklahoma Territory learned that the famous Geronimo was now a prisoner living nearby. One of them got the idea to put Geronimo on display. Surely, people would pay to see the famous old warrior. Their eyes glistened at the thought of how much money they could make.

So Geronimo became a traveling act, like a circus performer. He didn't have to do much to entertain the crowds. Just being himself was enough. His first journey was to the International Exposition in Omaha, Nebraska. There was a crowd of people at every place the train stopped, waiting to catch a glimpse of him. As shrewd as ever, Geronimo figured out a way to make money from them. At every stop he tore the buttons off of his jacket and sold them for twenty-five cents apiece. Of course, the buttons were snatched up by the excited crowd. Then, once the train was moving again, the old warrior would reach into a bag of buttons he had with him and carefully sew new ones on, ready for the next crowd.

The people who saw the quiet old Indian carefully dressed in white man's clothes had a hard time believing that he was once feared far and wide. But on one occasion their fear came out. Geronimo had gone with a few other Indians for a drive in the country outside of Omaha and they got lost amid the endless cornfields. When curfew time came and the Indians hadn't returned, a panic swept through the local people. By the time the Apaches finally found their way back, the streets were echoing with the cries of newsboys shouting: "Extra! Geronimo escapes! Apache murderers on their way back to Arizona!"

* * *

Geronimo made the most of his opportunity to see the white man's world. He carefully observed all the features of

American life. At the World's Fair the various acts amazed him. He watched a magician saw a woman in half, then saw her stand up unharmed. He was convinced that the magician had the Power. He also saw a trained polar bear. "I had never before seen a white bear," he said, impressed. He watched in shock as it obeyed the commands of its master. He decided that white bears were as smart as men, and much smarter than the grizzly bears he knew of. "I am sure that no grizzly bear could be trained to do these things," he said.

The amusement rides frightened him. He saw people getting into cars that slid down a waterfall, and heard their squeals of delight. This great, fearless warrior, who had faced death a thousand times, watched the action and remarked, "It looked too fierce for me."

But most of all he was impressed with how civilized the Americans behaved. "During all the time I was at the Fair no one tried to harm me in any way," he remarked with surprise. "Had this been among the Mexicans I am sure I should have been compelled to defend myself often." Even now, near the end of his life, he would not give up his hatred for Mexicans.

The height of Geronimo's fame came when he was invited to ride in the inauguration parade of President Theodore Roosevelt. For the occasion he dressed in full Apache costume, including a beautiful eagle-feather headdress. He rode on horseback beside chiefs from several other Indians tribes. But all eyes were on Geronimo. In fact, he was the most popular person in the whole parade, except, perhaps, for the new president.

Geronimo used his chance to meet with the president to push for his people's freedom. He addressed President Roosevelt as "Great Father," and told him solemnly, "White men are in the country that was my home. I pray you to tell them to go away and let my people go there and be happy.

"Great Father," he went on, "my hands are tied as with a rope. My heart is no longer bad. I will tell my people to obey no chief but the Great White Chief. I pray you to cut the ropes and make me free. Let me die in my own country, an old man who has been punished enough and is free."

But President Roosevelt could not agree to this. "There would be more war and more bloodshed," he told Geronimo. "It is best for you to stay where you are." He shrugged to show he was sorry. "That is all I can say, Geronimo, except that I am sorry, and have no feeling against you."

The American president, like the whole American nation, was beginning to push the "Indian problem" into the past. Thirty years earlier, the wars with various Indian tribes were the biggest news. Now the country had conquered the original inhabitants of America. Geronimo, the Apaches, and all the other Indians were people of the past. There were new problems, new challenges, and new frontiers ahead.

Alexander Graham Bell's telephone, invented thirty years before while Geronimo was rebelling against Indian Agent John Clum, was now in millions of homes. Americans could talk with people hundreds of miles away. The world was now moving faster and people demanded things to be done quickly.

Henry Ford had just begun to produce automobiles cheaply and quickly by using an assembly line of workers. The Ford Motor Company's Model T would soon be rolling through the streets. People were able to cover large distances in a remarkably short time.

Airplanes, motion pictures, phonograph records, and factories to make all these things were rapidly changing the way people lived. People's ideas about how they should live and what they should want in life were changing as well. The world of the Apaches, who lived so close to nature, suddenly seemed

Geronimo, Chihuahua, Nana, Loco, and Josanie while they were prisoners at Fort Sill, Oklahoma, July, 1895

terribly crude, old-fashioned, even silly. People were eager to stare at model Indian villages and wonder at how primitive the native Americans were.

When they were not on exhibit, the Apaches themselves continued to live dreary lives on the Oklahoma reservation. They were still prisoners and their children continued to die. Old Geronimo, now close to eighty, watched his tribe dwindle and wept tears of frustration. "We are vanishing from the earth," he said sadly, "yet I cannot think we are useless or Usen would not have created us."

At this time Geronimo dictated the memoirs of his life to a young schoolteacher who lived nearby. He told of his earliest memories, of hanging in a cradle and gazing out on the sights of the tipi village of the Bedonkohe Apaches. He told of his youth and of the traditional ways of his people. He recounted his first test as a warrior, the raids on Mexico, and the terrible massacre at Janos where his wife, mother, and children were killed.

He detailed the long years of warfare between the Apaches and the Americans. He told of the wisdom of Mangas Coloradas and Cochise, and the bravery of Victorio. And he recounted his final surrender to General Miles and the years of frustration in the East. He ended his autobiography with yet another plea to President Roosevelt to return the Apaches to Arizona. "It is my land," he wrote, "my home, my fathers' land, to which I now ask to be allowed to return. I want to spend my last days there, and be buried among those mountains. If this could be I might die in peace, feeling that my people, placed in their native homes, would increase in numbers, rather than diminish as at present, and that our name would not become extinct."

As Geronimo talked about his life, a middle-aged Apache translated his words into English for the schoolteacher. This Apache was none other than Daklugie, the child Geronimo's sister Ishton had almost died giving birth to, when Geronimo went into the mountains to ask Usen to help the Apache babies grow. The old man sat telling of his long life to the one who was once a sign that the Apaches would continue to live. But that sign was not proving to be true. The Apache people were captive and steadily dying.

On an icy evening in February, 1909, Geronimo rode alone from the reservation to a nearby town on business. His heart was filled with sadness. He knew his own end was near, and he feared that the end of his entire tribe was also coming. Against regulations he bought a bottle of whisky and, in his sadness, drank himself into a stupor. Late that night the ancient Indian rode homeward unsteadily. On the way he fell off his horse and

Geronimo

landed in a watery ditch. By the time he was found the next morning he was desperately ill. Three days later, with Daklugie and several other devoted Apaches at his bedside, old Geronimo died.

But Usen's promise to Geronimo was not completely false. The Chiricahua Apaches themselves did not quite die out. Three years after Geronimo's death, in 1912, the United States Congress freed them from captivity. After that the Apaches split into two groups. Some chose to remain on a new site in Oklahoma and there they created farms and settled at long last into a free, stable life.

The other group was granted space on the reservation of another Apache tribe, the Mescaleros, in the beloved hills of New Mexico. On a spring morning in 1913, 183 Apaches returned to their native land. In the little group was the warrior Naiche, son of Cochise, who was now an old man himself. Daklugie and his family also went. Perhaps the oldest of the whole group was Dostehseh, daughter of Mangas Coloradas and wife of Cochise, who had served food to Geronimo and Cochise when they sat down to plan war on the Mexicans.

As the twentieth century moved forward, many of the Apaches who stayed in Oklahoma adopted a modern way of life. They chose to live in houses and learned trades. Some became printers, blacksmiths, modern farmers. Others moved away and got jobs in big cities like Chicago and Detroit, far from the Apache homeland.

Most of those who returned to their homeland in the Southwest stayed, and their families are there still. They work in lumber mills, on cattle ranches, or as tour guides. They still sing the old Apache songs and dance the traditional dances. And at night the young sit with wide eyes listening to the creation story. Once again the tale is told of the battle between the birds and the beasts, and of the boy Apache, who founded a great race and wore the eagle's feathers on his head to honor the noble bird.

Now cars buzz past the Apache homes, and jets fly overhead, and they no longer hunt in the mountains for food. But Geronimo's people are alive and well. As he did long ago, Apache children still gaze into the star-filled sky every evening and thank Usen, the maker of all things, for giving them a land that is perfect for them. Geronimo's fear that the Apaches would die out has not come true.

Suggested Reading

Brown, Dee. *Bury My Heart at Wounded Knee: An [ ] dian History of the American West*. New York: Holt, Rine[ ] & Winston, 1974.

Josephy, Alvin M., Jr. *The Patriot Chiefs*, New York: Viking P[ ] 1961.

Wyatt, Edgar. *Geronimo: The Last Apache War Chief*. New Y[ ] McGraw-Hill Book Company, Inc., 1952.

ADVANCED READING:

Barrett, S.M. *Geronimo's Story of His Life*, New York: E.P. Dut[ ] 1970, newly edited by Fredrick W. Turner, III.

Betzinez, Jason and W.S. Nye. *I Fought with Geronimo*, Harrisb[ ] PA: Stackpole, 1960.

Bourke, John G. *An Apache Campaign in the Sierra Madre*, N[ ] York: Scribners, 1958.

Clum, Woodworth. *Apache Agent, the Story of John P. Clum*, [ ] ton: Houghton Mifflin, 1936.

SUGGESTED READING

Cremony, John C. *Life Among the Apaches,* Lincoln, NB: University of Nebraska Press, 1983.

Davis, Britton. *The Truth About Geronimo,* Chicago: Lakeside Press, 1951.

Debo, Angie. *Geronimo: The Man, His Life, His Time,* Norman, OK: University of Oklahoma Press, 1976.

Thrapp, Dan L. *The Conquest of Apacheria,* Norman, OK: University of Oklahoma Press, 1975.